GOD'S HIDDEN PLACES

GOD'S HIDDEN PLACES

Patricia P. Gallagher

God's Hidden Places

Copyright © 2024 by Patricia P. Gallagher. All rights reserved.

No part of this publication may be reproduced, stored in a retrieval system or transmitted in any way by any means, electronic, mechanical, photocopy, recording or otherwise without the prior permission of the author except as provided by USA copyright law.

The opinions expressed by the author are not necessarily those of URLink Print and Media.

1603 Capitol Ave., Suite 310 Cheyenne, Wyoming USA 82001
1-888-980-6523 | admin@urlinkpublishing.com

URLink Print and Media is committed to excellence in the publishing industry.

Book design copyright © 2024 by URLink Print and Media. All rights reserved.

Published in the United States of America

Library of Congress Control Number: 2024914378
ISBN 978-1-68486-835-3 (Paperback)
ISBN 978-1-68486-836-0 (Digital)

10.07.24

CONTENTS

Dedication vii
Acknowledgements..ix
Preface..xi
Introduction..xv
Chapter 1: The Journey Unfolds..........................1
Chapter 2: Crazy-Awfully-Terribly Different......17
Chapter 3: Is That All There Is? 21
Chapter 4: Color Blind 28
Chapter 5: The Miracle Parish 36
Chapter 6: The Voice That Could Never
Be Dismissed....................................39
Chapter 7: Holding My Breath 45
Chapter 8: Parallel Positions..............................49
Chapter 9: A Goodbye Letter............................55
Chapter 10: What the Hell! 60
Chapter 11: Sanctuary/My Sanctuary 63
Chapter 12: A Screaming Cry of a
Motherless Woman 68

PART II: AWAKENING

Chapter 13: Universal Cracking In Us All............77

Chapter 14: Mother Earth Answers Our Longings 82

Chapter 15: Pickled Cucumbers 87

Chapter 16: The Fragrance of a Feminine Spirit....93

Chapter 17: Never -Never Land...........................97

Chapter 18: Unlimited Possibilities.....................104

Chapter 19: The Hidden Milk of Everlastingness 112

Epilogue..117

DEDICATION

I wish to dedicate this book to all my 11 grandchildren and 3 great-granddaughters as they become our future lightworkers, moving us into the joy and peace humanity deserves.

ACKNOWLEDGEMENTS

Writing a book about your life is most definitely a surreal process. I couldn't have finished this book without the support of so many.

I want to thank my muse, Helena, not only for her guidance, but also for her gentle pushes to lead me to completion. My monthly encounters with her and her wife Gail led to a sisterhood that I didn't see coming, but now experience as a continuous sense of joy within, knowing that this connection will last into an eternal future.

I want to thank Nicloe. You were my right hand sitting with me for hours as I exposed you to my first draft and on... Inspiring me to keep writing even when I didn't think I knew how to carry so much information onto a page. Your investigative eye, heart and mind didn't let even a comma go by, much less a floating thought of mine that required grounding for others to understand. You were my constant strength and I thank you with all my heart.

I want to thank Marie who introduced me to Helena, allowing this book to begin with integrity and a blessing of fulfillment. Thank you for leading me to an angel. And thank you for finding the title of my book after just reading the second of many drafts. Most importantly, thank you for your love as we continue to grow in tender awareness of each other.

I want to thank my spiritual gathering group, my spiritual family who watched my channeling grow at our meetings and in my writings. Without this community this book wouldn' have had a chance of being written. Beth, Joanne, Joyce, Nicole and Wayne, I love you all!

I want to thank my family who had the patience to bear with my having to leave them for a time to write in seclusion. Jean, Vel and Charlie I thank you for all you've given me with love.

I want to thank Maddy for her presence for six months as I agonized over getting this book to the right publisher. And how graciously she endured my mood swings, while I nit-picked through every line to complete this writing. Thank you for your monetary aid allowing this book to go to market. I am grateful beyond words for your tremendous support and love.

Lastly, I want to thank all those who touched my life and want to say here, please forgive any hurt I've done intentionally or unintentionally in my many years, as I also forgive anyone who has hurt me intentionally or unintentionally. Only love will set us free.

PREFACE

This is a brilliant and poignant book by a modern mystic whose clear voice emerges out of contemporary confusion and complexity.

If you are already familiar with mysticism this book is a banquet for the soul. If you are not yet aware of the eons of mystical thinking and writings, of seeking truths beyond visible reality, Reverend Gallagher introduces us to a profound world of spiritual consciousness.

Even in early Childhood, Reverend Gallagher was aware of being called by Spirit for a specific purpose in the world. She casts a wide invitation to her readers to join her, "and experience the consciousness of a universal Love." She became a seeker, driven by an "ache that has never left me" to be "as close to God as possible." At age eleven she wrote a poem she channeled on her way to church and school every morning.

I love you God, indeed I do

The pain in my heart shows you

Born and educated in Catholicism, she could hear God's voice within her even as a child. Always it called her to the priesthood which had no place for her. Later she was in a loving marriage, mother of three children, yet the calling did not diminish. It became a Force that could not be ignored. Is it any wonder that such intensity found release through addiction. She speaks of lost years in and out of rehab. After her children had grown, she found her priesthood in the Episcopal Church. Then, after approximately five years of study, she was ordained. Yet ordination did not resolve that pain of separation from God. It was then she realized the "discovery of self" was necessary in order to discover God. Thus, her search for God and wholeness continued and deepened in her service as an Episcopal priest for seventeen years. She moved on to missions in Hospice and Bereavement Counseling.

Still the voice continued, calling her now to understand and teach the Nature of God. In that endeavor, could she perhaps also be revealed to God and to herself? Questions crowded in her mind. Is God also a seeker? Is God's quest the same quest as our own? The ancient question emerges once more. "Why am I here? "Who am I?" Am I part of God as God's Spirit is part of me? These questions led her to imagine thinking across dimensions into the vastness of universal consciousness in the new accelerated reality of our contemporary world.

The intricate journey Reverend Gallagher describes is one of both Pain and Elation, Mystery and

Insight. In that turning point she also understood the Alpha and Omega, Beginning and End, complete each other.

Preface written by Helena J. Sturnick, PhD

Author of <u>Fire in the Soul</u>, a personal narrative of the goddess Sekmet's Years of Dream Teaching with her.

INTRODUCTION

How should I start this book so you don't leave me after the first page?

Instead wanting to run your fingers through my words, nestle in my thoughts and find meaningful moments to fill the seeking of your soul.

Will you stay with me as you settle into the sea of your dreams and the cracks in your heart?

Where you can be touched by the radical love that can only be felt by the kiss of angels.

And experience the consciousness of a universal love?

We are all in this together.

Come and feel the moment.

Come and feel the vibration.

Bring your baggage so you can put it down.

Bring your wide-eyed expectations so you can envision a new creation.

Come and see this new creation with me.

Come and see yourself.

You are me and I am you.

I do pray, as you walk through this book, it trips you and you fall into the heart of your soul.

Let us begin.

CHAPTER 1
The Journey Unfolds

Many years ago, at the age of eleven, when my heart felt an ache and my whole being was set afire, I started writing poetry. I became a seeker and that ache has never left me, even in my darkest hours.

I love you God indeed I do
The pain in my heart shows you.

I began my studies in the Catholic school system taught by nuns. I yearned to be as close to God as possible. I walked to church every morning before school to go to Mass and receive Holy Communion. I believed that if I swallowed the host, I would feel closer to my God. I could hear God's voice inside me during those young years and later heard it calling me to the priesthood. I married and had three children, but always had a persistent voice in the back of my mind pushing me to pursue ordination. Oh, but where to go with this in the Roman Catholic Church, a woman was sure to wonder!

A few years later I was introduced to the Episcopal Church where, for the first time, I saw a woman consecrating and saying Mass. I joined the church and that same woman mentored me as I started my ordination process of five years. After seminary and ordination, I was given my first parish and became priest-in-charge of many parishes over 17 years. I felt complete as I answered my calling. I thought I had it all, motherhood and priesthood! I didn't realize how wrong I was, there was so much more.

Approximately seven years later, after my ordination, my children were grown and out of the house. I was taken beyond the teachings of traditional Christianity through my readings and experiences in meditation. I experienced different levels of knowledge and new insights. Thus began another journey into new worlds, leading me onward to Christian Existentialism, Buddhism and Taoism, New Thought Churches and Spiritualism. I secretly trained with Brian Weiss to become a past life regression therapist and watched movies like "What the Bleep" and "The Secret," believing that I had stepped beyond the boundaries of my priesthood and the bishop's liking. I learned about manifesting and the world of quantum physics and channeling. I began to see the connection between science and religion. A new and incredible world was opening up to me and I was obsessed with all of it. Some years later, after bouts of alcoholism, drug abuse and divorce, I finally came out as a lesbian. I was given 40 acres of land with a house in Connecticut from a fellow who knew of me through a colleague. There, my partner and I began a non-profit spiritual life center, we called "Shepardfields." It was open to all, with a specialized ministry to the LGBTQ+ community.

Eleven years later, I retired from parish work to pursue a deep calling to hospice work, though still and always under the auspices of the Episcopal Church and the Bishop. As a hospice chaplain and bereavement counselor, I learned and grew immensely from being present with those who were transitioning and their loved ones.

After several more years, I felt that this chapter was coming to a close and wondered what the Universe had in store for me next. Soon enough, The National Spiritual Alliance Spiritualist Church, that I had been exploring, approached me to become their interim minister. I accepted with little hesitation…

Whoa, await a minute. I should stop here and tell you what really transpired -- so you can see how a life, my life in this particular story, full of agony, foolishness, and "hellraising" passions could ever lead to one of secure inner peace. How the discovery of self can lead one to true empowerment, and the ability to choose love and gratitude over fear and separation in every moment. So first, let us meet the little girl who started all this.

Meet Cookie

Hi, my name is Cookie. Well, it's really Patricia Marie Elizabeth Gallagher but that's so long I think that's why my parents gave me the nickname Cookie. I've got a brother named Donald Hector Patrick Paul Gallagher and I almost can't breathe after trying to say his whole name, and he doesn't even have a nickname. We live with our parents in a big city called Manhattan. We're on the 4th floor of an eleventh story building in what is called a project. A project has hundreds of tall buildings, all the same with a little grass and trees around them so they don't just look like giant boxes with windows. We have playgrounds and playground teachers who teach us games and stuff. We got skully, roly-poly, hopscotch, monkey bars, baby swings, big kid swings for us, and two great big painted circles for circle games. Our playground is number 4 out of 11 so, when someone asks us where we live, we don't say 277 Avenue C on 23rd Street. No. Heck, nobody would know where that is, we just say, "Playground 4, meet you there."

"Uh-oh my mom's calling me. I'm late for dinner. I'll meet you down in playground 4 at six, bye." Oh, by the way, I'm eleven years old and everybody calls me a tomboy cause I'm just one of the guys.

Who the heck is this kid?

"6x6 equals 36,
6x7 equals 42,
6x8 equals …"

"Hey, Cookie, you must be a chocolate chip cookie with all those freckles."

6x10 equals 60,
6x11 equals 66,
6x12 equals …"

"Hey Philip you're a meat-head and…"

"Patricia, you and Philip will stay after school today and write I will not talk during class 100 times."

Oh, that Philip, that meatball, I can't believe he's making us miss the most important circle games of the year. We stayed after school writing for what seemed like a century.

"I WILL NOT TALK DURING CLASS."
"I WILL NOT TALK DURING CLASS."
"I WILL NOT TALK DURING CLASS."

Finally, I heard Sister Christopher say,

"Alright you can both go home now, and Miss Gallagher, you can walk me home to the convent."

"Yes, Sister, may I carry your bag, Sister?" We were all taught to ask, as that was the polite and respectful thing to do.

"Thank you, Pat. I loved your poem."

I love you God, indeed I do

The pain in my heart shows you.

"I'm beginning to think you're a little mystic, going to church every morning and writing poems. I want to tell you a secret that I shouldn't be telling. I want you to know I feel a special connection with you, but you have to promise me you won't tell anyone. Okay, the last name I was born with was Gallagher, and I see so much of myself in you it's hard to believe."

I felt so special I just wanted to hug my Sister Christopher and kiss her!

"Well Patricia, I guess I'll take my bag now and while you're here, go in and ask Sister Agnita if she needs you to do any errands with her."

"Hey Cookie, where have you been? You missed the best circle games. Our playground 4 clobbered playground 9. We knocked them dead!"

"Great, well I'll see you after school tomorrow, Bernadette."

"Hey Cookie, what happened? Did you get in trouble at school?"

"I gotta go. See you tomorrow, bye!"

Meet Cookie's Boyfriend

"Hi, Cookie!"

"Oh, hi Jimmie."

"Are you going home now?"

"Yeah."

"Well, ahh, can I walk with you?"

"Sure, I don't care. Come on."

"Uh, hey, uh…can I carry your books?"

"What? What do ya mean carry my books? I can carry my own books! You're weird Jimmy. You're really weird. See you later."

You know, that crazy Jimmy? He did that for the next week. He kept asking me if he could carry my books. Did he think I was a nun or what? I finally said,

"Well, if that's what you want to do Jimmy, here, go ahead and do it, take my books!"

And he did. He walked me home every day carrying those couple of books, looking like he was just so fine. You know what else? When Jimmie and I were walking home one day, I saw this guy staring at us and I said,

"Jimmie, look at that guy staring at us. What a creep, what a creep! You know we should stick out our tongues or something."

"Cookie, what's the matter with you? Don't you think he might be lookin' at you cause he thinks you're pretty?"

Pretty! I never thought I was pretty. I never thought of that question at all. I think Jimmie's super. You know what? I think, I like this, Jimmy. I don't know. I kinda like walking home from school with him. He asked me to go steady the other day and I think I'm going to say yes.

Sunday morning came only two days later. Sister Thomas had a big bell in her hand as usual this Sunday morning.

"Ding-a-ling — Ding-a-ling!

"Quiet! Quiet everyone, it's time to line up now". She pointed, "First grade here, second grade here." And to the higher grades, "You all know where to stand. Now let's move on, children. It's almost nine o'clock and we have to take our seats for Mass."

"Hey Cookie."

"Hi, Jimmie."

"You look nice in a dress. Why don't you wear a dress more? The only time I see you in a dress is on Sunday mornings for church."

"Boy Jimmie, that's the dumbest question you've asked so far. How could I run, play punch ball, skully or ring-o'-leary-o', and all the other games we play at the playground if I'm wearing a sissy girl's dress?"

"Well, I guess you're right. I've been thinking, if I get enough money together to take you out to see a movie or something, well…uh…do you think maybe you'd consider wearing a dress then?"

"Well, maybe. Tell you what. If you and me walked out the front way instead of the playground way, the guys wouldn't see us and then well, maybe…yes."

"Oh, great and then I'll wear my sports jacket and a tie."

"Are you going to pay for both of us?"

"Sure."

"But, that's a lot of money, Jimmie."

"Nay, the boy's supposed to do that when he's going steady, ya know."

"Oh, wow that's great! Could we get popcorn too?"

Sister Christopher cut in, "Patricia and Jimmie get in line now, everyone's already walking in."

"Yes, Sister Christopher, we didn't notice."

"Now don't run, walk. Remember when you ran last week, Patricia, and tripped and fell in the mud? I had to take you into the ladies room and wash your legs."

Oh my God, I'm so embarrassed!!! Did she have to say that in front of Jimmie? It was bad enough having it happen in front of half the school. I think I'm going to die standing right here on this very spot!

"So, walk Patricia, but hurry."

Jimmie and I couldn't sit together at Mass because the girls sit on one side of the church and the boys sit on the other side. I've gotta confess in the confessional this week that I didn't do much praying this Sunday morning. Instead, I was thinking about Jimmie and how much fun it'll be going out on my first date with him. I just sat in that pew and dreamt through the whole Mass. I did tell God I was sorry later for not giving him his special time. And you know what? I think He understood. And you know what else? I think He's still my highest friend.

Patricia P. Gallagher

Cookie's First Date

"Ma, Ma! I can't find the hairbrush… Ma, Ma! I can't find the belt to my dress…

Ma, Ma! I can't…"

"Wait, hold on, slow down young lady, you're getting yourself all hot and bothered.

Let me help you."

"But Jimmie will be here in twenty minutes Ma, and I've got to look my very best self.

I'm so excited Ma and I feel so grown up all of a sudden. How do I look Ma?"

"Like a princess" my father's deep voice said, surprising me.

" Daddy, you're home!"

I rushed into his outstretched arms and he picked me up and repeated, "Yes, just like a princess and that's why I named you Patricia, so I could call you Princess Pat. And now my lovely daughter, you even look like a Princess. I guess I'll have to talk with this young man and make sure he knows that you're still my girl first."

"Ah, Daddy, I love you."

"Ding-Dong!"

"Daddy, quick! Put me down! I've got to get my coat. Bye Mom - bye Dad!"

"What movie are we going to see, Jimmie? Oh, here comes our bus."

"Go ahead of me Cookie."

"No, you should go first Jimmy. You said you're paying for the bus too."

"Yes, but the girl always goes first."

"Really? I guess I don't know much about these girl-boy rules."

"That's okay, it makes you more fun to be with."

Ya know, at the movie, Jimmy helped me take my coat off. When we were sitting watching the big screen, he put his arm around my shoulder the whole movie. He didn't move an inch and neither did I for the whole movie. My back was breaking and his arm must have been broken too. Wow, these first dates aren't as easy as I thought they'd be. But we had fun. After the movie we decided not to take the bus home but instead, get two slices of pizza and walk. It was a long walk, and we held hands all the way home. I had warm feelings all over me that day, just like I have when God talks to me, and I never wanted it to end.

The Wall

"Mom, mom! Mrs. Risso is knocking on the wall again, should I take the message for you?"

"Yes!"

"Okay, I'll knock back to let her know we're listening."

My mom and Mrs. Risso were next door neighbors and they had worked out codes together. This code meant that Mrs. Risso wanted to know if we had some coffee. We did, so my mom went in to give her some. You see, at this point, Mrs. Risso was very sick.

She was in a wheelchair so my mom went to her most of the time now. It wasn't fun anymore to play what Mary and I used to call *"the wall game."* Because now even when Mary and I knocked on the wall, it was because her mother needed something or because the Monsignor was coming to bring Holy Communion. Then Mary and I were needed to greet him at the door holding tall lit white candles in big gold holders. We would walk in front of Monsignor until we got to the table which Mary had prepared like an altar. Then, we would put the candles down on opposite ends of the table and Monsignor would say Mass and give Mrs. Risso, Mary and myself Holy Communion. It was quite a thrill for us to act like altar boys. It made us feel so important and made me feel closer to God. We loved him, as did most of the kids in our school and that even made us feel more important.

Mary's mothers knocks grew fainter every week and the knocks now never created a message, just one or two knocks for help and my mother would run in. Sometimes, my mom had to help Mrs. Risso off the floor where she had fallen trying to walk as she used to, by holding on to furniture or the wall. But now she couldn't because her legs were too weak to hold her. Another time my mom ran to help her off the toilet, because her arms had become too weak for her to get herself from her wheelchair to the toilet and back. It was so scary and sad that I didn't know how to say what was inside me. And then, her neck became too weak to hold her head up. And there were no more knocks on our wall cause Mrs. Risso was always in bed. My mom would help take care of Mrs. Risso with some kind of nurse and she did all the housework too. Mary and I continued to play together until her father got home and then he would take over everything.

I liked Mr. Risso, he was always gentle and kind to me, but every time I looked at him now, his eyes were so sad and he didn't smile or laugh like he used to. As a matter of fact, the whole apartment with everyone in it, including my mother, seemed to look different and even smell different. Sometimes, I didn't like going in and would invite Mary to play in my apartment. But most of the time, we'd play at Mary's because she didn't want to leave her mom. I didn't know anything about dying or how houses or people got ready for the process, but that's what was happening. And then the day came when there was no more seeing and visiting Mrs. Risso. There was no more knocking for me to get my candle and come to help serve Monsignor. There was no more Monsignor coming. I didn't know what to say to Mary. I didn't know what to say to myself. I prayed to God last night to please not take my mom. And help Mary find another mom, or she can share mine. It was sure all right with me.

Cookie's First Fight

"Ah, c'mon Chris, don't be like that, race me. You're the fastest in our playground and I have to get ready for our Junior Olympics next week. All the playgrounds will be competing for the gold medal and I don't want to be the one to have our playground lose."

"Well, okay Cookie, and if you even come close to beating me, you'll beat any girl in New York City, never mind all the playgrounds!"

"Yeah, OK, sure Mr. Big. Am I supposed to kiss your feet before we start too? We'll race from here to the end of the playground and back. Ha! OK? Mark, get set, GO!"

Everyone was shouting. "Go Cookie!'

"Go Chris!"

"Show 'em girls are better!"

"Don't let a girl beat you!"

"Go-Go-Go!!!"

"Tie, it's a tie! What a race!"

"Yeah Cookie, playground 4 has this one in the bag. You can beat any girl in any playground!"

Then Joey adds, "Oh yeah that was just lucky. My brother let you tie so you'd feel good."

"Cut it out Joey!"

"Says who, Bernadette? You going to make me? And Cookie your mother's a
#**#**!"

"What, my mother? Nobody talks about my mother! Joey, I'm gonna…"

Joey took off. I guess he saw how mad my eyes were. I was so angry. I took off right behind him. We ran for what seemed like a mile and then I caught him from behind. He fell. I jumped on top of him, feeling crazy cause I was so mad and not really knowing what I was doing. I held his arms down with my knees and raised my left hand (being lefthanded, you know) making a fist ready to hit Joey square in the face. Then something hit me instead, and I realized what I was doing. I said, "Joey, you take that back about my mother and never say anything like it again, and I'll let you up and you can go home." His face was so red and his breathing was so hard and his eyes so afraid, he couldn't even speak. But he shook his head 'yes' and I got up and let him go.

As I was standing there, I had a horrible feeling in my stomach like when your mom is ashamed of you for something bad you've done. Well, I'm not sure I did something so bad, but I felt that same sick stomach and my mom wasn't even near me. But I did realize something new about myself that day, without my mom or anyone even having to tell me and it felt good. I realized I could never hurt anyone and I never, ever wanted to!

CHAPTER 2

Crazy-Awfully-Terribly Different

My high school years were awkward. I had two groups of girlfriends. One group was in the honors class, so I guess some would call them a little nerdy and a bit boring. The other group could care less about being book smart and liked taking risks and fooling around all the time. I liked hanging out with both, although I didn't feel like I totally fit in with either group. I didn't feel smart enough for the first group, though somewhere in the back of my mind I knew I was. And in the other group, I loved joking around and getting into mischief with them, but I also knew that I was so crazy, awfully, terribly different.

All I truly wanted was to know God more clearly, as I had this passion, this burning passion inside me that wouldn't let go. In these teenage years, when popular songs were playing and we were all singing along with them like:

"To Know, know, know him is to love, love, love, him and I do, and I do, and I do"

I was only thinking about God of course, pretending that I was thinking about boys, or for that matter girls, even though I was not aware as yet. I guess I could say my whole life was a magical fairy land starting with my birth that never should have happened, but did following my mother's three miscarriages. While on complete bed rest she prayed for a second miracle of life. She called me her tiniest magical experience and when I look back thinking: magical/mystical…magical/mystical…hmm…Oh, maybe she was right!

When I was in my senior year, I decided I wanted to be a nun as I knew the priesthood was out of the question in my church. My Spanish teacher agreed and started preparing me to meet the mother superior of the Sisters of Charity. In the middle of my Senior year, I went for my interview and received my first real blow and biggest rejection. I was not to be received as a postulant in the order of the Sisters of Charity. I was told I was too young and immature and to return in a few years. I was devastated and felt abandoned by my God.

As the years passed, instead of going back I fell in love and married. I had three precious bundles of joy stare into my eyes. This allowed me to experience the first looks into the divinity of humanity in each of these newborns faces. I fell in love with every beat of their hearts and every cell in their bodies. It took my breath away as I saw the universe in miniature and my soul knelt in gratitude! How could I be so worthy?

In the years to follow, nagging thoughts of joining the priesthood continued to hound me with other thoughts relentlessly pressing in, as to who I really was. During those years alcohol and drugs became my go to comforts as I laid in the darkness of despair.

After these insane times, in and out of two rehab facilities and having a near death experience, writing became my comfort. So did spending time among people like myself, who were also in AA, or later on, were part of various spiritual groups that I joined.

Maybe, it was within the first rehab days, that my writing truly began, as I started with:

I Was Once a Magician

I was once a magician,

I drank to create illusions and played tricks with my imagination.

I had a unique sleight of hand - waving my hand over the pills - now you see them, now you don't.

My death-defying acts were simply superlative; my audiences went wild when I sawed my feelings in half and drowned my reason in a tank.

My bag of tricks ranged from breathing fire to smoking joints, and my costume was one of many masks.

My alcoholism and cross addiction were a daily show of morbid magic acts and at the finale ... I was caught holding the bag.

CHAPTER 3
Is That All There Is?

My demons came flooding back after a few months of sobriety, and I found myself yet again in a second rehab facility wishing I were dead. Upon entering, I was administered a dose of Librium and my vital signs were taken as a general course of starting my rehabilitation process. I was having trouble sleeping that first evening and was given a very mild sedative, and went to my room to lie down for the night. I woke up to go to the bathroom and had trouble shaking off the medication. I held onto the walls for balance as I walked down the hall. All I can remember was entering the women's bathroom and coming out, falling into the strong arms of a tall man. He had been watching me walk the hall, recognizing that I was in some kind of distress. This gentle giant sat me down at the nurse's station and the nurse asked him, what my pulse was. I could barely hear this nurse's aid's response. "Can you believe it's ten!" as I began gasping for air and slumping over. I was told later, that as the nurse was preparing an adrenaline shot, she asked him again for a reading on my pulse and he responded with an "eight".

During this interval I was not aware of my situation. Instead, I was pleasantly going through a dark tunnel-like experience. I saw a light approaching and a group of formless beings in robes and hoods appearing, somewhat like monks in an intense conversation. I was stopped in this suspended animation and told, or somehow understood, that I was not to join them, but rather return back as I had more to do.

I was immediately transported back into my body gasping for air, as the nurse was coming at me with another adrenaline shot. Suddenly, I lurched forward and began breathing again. I was put to bed and woke feeling nauseous with a good-sized headache and an anger to fit both these ailments. The next three to four days I was very weak and could not eat anything except a little soup now and again.

I can vividly remember those days sitting there feeling the worst hangover with a rage forming within me. I could not continue, not allowed to go deeper in that other-worldly experience beyond those monk-like figures. Not allowed to continue to go into that dimension of peace, that far surpassed anything here. I knew I had to come back for my precious three little ones, but beyond that I didn't know what else I had returned for.

Each day I sat in silence with this rage inside me and with the pain of failing. During those days I was always taken to the same comfortable chair, across from the same man playing cards, and a blanket was gently placed on my lap. So, after a few days, I became curious about this man and I asked him:

"You look so comfortable here. How many times have you been in this place?"

He said, "Oh honey, I'm not sure but I can't count them on my fingers anymore."

Oh my god, that hit me like a ton of bricks, as I started to hear Peggy Lee singing in my head:

"Is that all there is, is that all there is

If that's all there is, my friend, then let's keep dancing.

Let's break out the booze and have a ball

If that's all there is."

And this is when my life changed. My rage began to settle into anger; my anger into acceptance, and my acceptance into peace as my whole being knew it was over. I wasn't going to dance this dance again, and this card playing Irish guy, still with a twinkle in his eyes saved my life.

I so wanted to meet up with this man again after I had been sober for a time. I wanted to thank him for saving my life, but I didn't even know his name and never saw him at any AA meeting in my area. Many years later I happened to venture out of my area with friends to a different AA meeting. While walking in and finding a chair, I happened to look back a few rows and there he was! I couldn't wait until that meeting was over. Rushing to meet him, where he sat among some friends, I blurted out, "Finally, I get to see you again! I know you probably don't remember me, but I prayed for years that I would meet you again to thank you for saving my life!"

He said, "I do remember you. You were the lady who came back from the dead at the rehab center. And honey, I'm glad I could save your life because I sure can't save mine!"

He got up and walked out, without that twinkle in his eyes, and I never saw or heard about him again as sadness enveloped my being.

After that second rehab struggle and having had a near-death experience, I found myself sitting with pen in hand. I was writing what seemed to be flowing not from me, but through me. The script that followed ignited within me a complete and final breakthrough! It filled me with the breath of serenity my soul so hungered for and drinking became a thing of my past. Here is how that script read:

There Again - Back Again

As I walked away from time, I was propelled uncontrollably by the bottle. The world stripped from me, as I began once again to lay helplessly naked as its prey.

I could feel the tingling sensuous rush of the first drink and where it took me beyond.

I felt as though someone was unchaining me, thrusting me into freedom, exclaiming, "You can have your misery back anytime." As I laughed to myself, the relentless compulsion was drawing its first breath after many hours of confinement. And my fields of dawn were turning into fields of darkness. The light was fading, my feelings becoming unknown even to myself. My memories quickening from virtuous to vile, reluctantly remembering the little girl found once again, the little girl lost. How savage a freedom can this be? A wall must be built, defenses must be cemented in and the intellect must be buried. I must trust no one. I must protect only me.

As the "me" became bigger and bigger, I stumbled and wandered aimlessly in states of unending confusion. The wall confused me, the drink confused me and I fell into addiction mercilessly. Where was I in these moments of insanity? I thought I unlocked the chains and stepped onto a new planet with no holes to fall into, no one to answer to, no one but… me. Loneliness again became the winner.

How do I get through, get back into time? Trapped. The monkey on my back, who was really unchained, was growing all this time now looking down on me. Chained by it, I became a slave, and my freedom a fleeting fantasy. The more I cried to be unchained the tighter the chains of compulsion and pride choked me. My pride would spit water on the flames, only to madden my ego and set it onto bigger and better trips…a prisoner of self.

Fighting, tiring, falling, drinking, fighting, tiring, falling, I surrendered and asked for help, knowing nothing more was required of me to make my new beginning. Growth could start again. Despair could become hope, and the little girl lost now, once again could seek the little girl found.

The wall can be patiently dis-assembled with care. For as a child, pain cannot be understood for too long and attention spans are short. And, those words that some people never say, but as children wait to be told, I'll also need at each turning point…I love you.

When will I ever find what's on the tip of my mind? Maybe today, maybe tomorrow, but never any of those yesterdays. Before I die, I do so want to touch the WOMAN I could be.

During the next several years as I was realizing that I had to surrender to who I was to stop the pounding in my heart. I could feel the dark night of the soul creeping upon me as I fought the denial of being a drunk, and the awareness of being a lesbian; all culminating in the swirl of the initial call to the priesthood. People say there is no place called hell, hell is on Earth. And believe me, this is where I was taken and felt left to burn in the fires of my own making. What the "hell" was I to do now? I had joined AA, found a spiritual guide in the habit of a devoted Dominican cloistered nun. Later I divorced my husband, the father of my children, whom I loved dearly as a companion. And I fell in love with a woman. God help me, for as a good Catholic I surely was damned! I was never to divorce, and never to leave the church, and a woman! So, if indeed, as the church expounds, there is a hell, I felt I had already joined the ranks.

I wondered in this darkened place, where is the light that I might chase?

I touch, I smell, I hear but cannot see,

Ahh, but then I turn round and there…is me.

After ten years of intense, and at times crippling meanderings within the depths of my soul, I finally came around to asking myself, "What have I come here to do?" Knowing the answer since early childhood, it certainly was not hard to speak: "A priest my dear self, a priest to be." I felt again this seeking rear its foolish head with an intense passion that was no stranger to me. I took up the adventure and the challenge. Always knowing that I would feel abnormal, and yet in some sort of way purified, driven to taste the next hidden piece of God. The next wonder of life to place upon my soul. I can't allow those pieces of fear to call me back, knowing that this pilgrimage will be a long and arduous one. But surely, little did I realize that "arduous" was such a calm word!!

CHAPTER 4

Color Blind

I am what I am

That's all that I can be.

Oh - well of course

Until I came to see. That you're a part of me, Heavens to be! I'm a part of you and You're a part of me.

Wow, is that what it's like Looking into eternity?

I wondered how I was supposed to start this ordination process. Exactly what would a seminary experience look or feel like? Who did I think I was, believing that I could become an Episcopal priest? How crazy, how insane!! I was about to drop this whole seemingly wild, misguided idea until the voice in my head shouted, "Take some seminary courses and begin!" Oh…. okay but where and how? I started searching for nondenominational seminaries on-line. I scrolled through many until I came across the New York Theological Seminary. The brakes screeched in my head as I came to a sudden stop. This seminary granted a part-time Masters of Divinity degree on weekends and week day evenings. Having grown up in that city, I knew I would feel at home with the people, and that it would take only two hours to travel by car. I was also aware that they had ample parking, so I wouldn't have to roam through dark city streets at night. Reading no further, and with almost no hesitation, I enrolled.

It was painful leaving my husband and children twice a week. Traveling four hours round trip in addition to the class time, would also prove to be quite a challenge. If it were not for the chance to traverse through the minds and hearts of others who also felt the same intense calling from within, it would have been too big a price to pay.

And so, it began. Kissing my family goodbye, suitcase in hand, I left for the required weekend orientation-retreat in upstate New York to begin my seminary experience.

Along with the other new students, I would meet the dean, associate dean, and their colleagues, in a comfortable and engaging environment.

After driving for some hours and having doubts about my wardrobe selection, I arrived at a breathtaking mansion. Was I at the right place? Parking the car and grabbing my bag, I walked up to a stately, massive architectural front door, flanked by two stunningly beautiful gas lanterns on each side. Though still somehow friendly and inviting, I thought again, "No way, this can't be it!" But very quickly, I was warmly greeted and shown to an exquisite winding staircase that led skyward in a graceful flowing arc to my room, on the floor above. There, I was to unpack and then promptly return downstairs to the common area for the meet and greet event.

Halfway up the stairs I stopped, slightly out of breath from the climb. I put my bag down and looked over the banister to notice a sea of people, where I assumed the meet and greet had already begun. I found myself holding my breath, in shock of what I was staring at! A woman came up behind me, huffing a bit, and took her place beside me. We turned to look at each other, both somewhat confused as to what we were observing. My stomach tightened, in immediate fear that I wouldn't be accepted here. The room was filled with people of color and we were the only white faces among them. My first thought was, "Whoa!" This must be how people of color felt, in this white society as a whole, and I was forced into a knowing that I had never before realized. I found myself kneeling within my being, asking for forgiveness for my insensitivity. While scanning my mind, I wondered just how many other white insensitivities I had. Was I a clueless racist?! And believe me when I say, I surely didn't have to contemplate this alone for very long. Our group discussions, held twice a week, brought these thoughts rushing towards me all too frequently. I found it true especially while engaging with one particular young black minister, who gave me no time to process and no time to respond. So, needless to say, I had an abundance of opportunities to ponder this question.

As the months rolled by, I became aware that I was sitting next to my mirrored whitefaced image less and less. I had become quite comfortable sitting anywhere within the group, except by that one particular young minister, who I felt despised me for being white.

I dug my intellectual claws into my studies and felt great satisfaction with my learnings. The ministry discussion groups, however, were another thing. I had never experienced such battles about hatred and racism in my white isolated life. I was attacked verbally, as were some others, but my attacks were different, since I was considered an ignorant white woman. Some of the words stabbed at me, creating knife-like wounds which bled deep within my soul, even though I was met with kindness and care from most. I can't recall any of the discussions verbatim, but I can tell you it was the most valuable, relevant, sacred and necessary time in my life, as I would carry these learnings forever in my heart and into all aspects of my ministry.

I can't explain how my shift in awareness happened, why it happened, or even when I felt it happen, but, it did indeed happen. One evening when I sat in class, I felt different inside. I realized I loved being there and I loved myself for accepting that I was a clueless racist. I now felt I had the courage to change by not staying in that ignorant state any longer. I felt a tremendous gratitude and pride for my colleagues, who led me out of my darkness into their light. They gave me a taste of their freedom to overcome. In turn that gave me my freedom to develop, reorientate and walk a fresh and advanced path.

I was now actually looking forward to our discussion groups, and instead of dreading what was being said to me or anyone, I could now hear where they were coming from because I was listening with a different ear. I felt their present and historic sufferings, flattened culture, and justifiable anger and rage. And thank God I got there when I did, as just a few weeks later in the middle of that semester, I was told that I had to go to Yale Divinity School for the rest of my seminary experience. I was accepted into the Episcopal ordination process that I had applied to some months before.

Now you would have thought I'd be elated and truly, I was, but I didn't want to leave my brothers and one sister who taught me how to love, how to be and live the school's motto - "Unity in Diversity", the one that had just penetrated my soul.

During the last group meeting, on the day I left, I sat in our familiar circle, tears already forming. In walked the dean and associate dean, to sit with us. They began by addressing me. I was completely humbled as they told me they were sorry to see me go. I felt a longing to stay, to finish out the year with them, to continue my inspiring growth. The group facilitator followed with his goodbye, and everyone in turn around the circle with their goodbyes. When it finally came to my young black minister, I was a bit fearful. He cleared his throat and said, "I have never said this to anyone before." I steeled myself for his remarks. "I can say for the first time in my life that I don't see you in color," and he stood up and we hugged and cried in each other's arms as he continued to say, "I too have learned so much from you". If I never hear anything about myself again, I know through him that I have come home in my soul. I realized that the only thing that matters is that we are all One in Love.

I left with hugs, flowers and tears of hope from all, for the future Reverend Patricia Gallagher. The next week I received my formal letter of acceptance from Yale Divinity School. It didn't begin to compare with the New York Theological Seminary, and the growth that I had just experienced there. Well, perhaps academically but not in heart and soul!

At Yale Divinity School, the ordination track had a multitude of bumps and turns. It took almost five years of jumping through numerous hoops, as we candidates put it. From an array of grueling committees, psychological testing, three years of seminary studies and a year of the diaconate, to name but a few. I spent many nights questioning if I had what it takes, while studying for my GOE's (General Ordination Exams) written and oral in each of six categories: Holy Scripture, Church History,

Christian Theology, Christian Ethics and Moral Theology, Liturgy and Church Music and the Theory and Practice of Ministry.

This became the most stressful arena of my life, as I was perched in front of a panel of priests and laity recalling endless details from deep within those subjects. I am still bewildered as to how I could have answered their questions without literally throwing-up on my shoes. When people say, "But for the grace of God…," that's truly what it was for me! Then again, the miraculous happened. On the feast of St. Bridget, February 1, 1991, as I knelt before God, the Bishop, family and friends, I took my vows of ordination as my dear old friend sang with all her heart:

"Here I am Lord

Is it I Lord?

I have heard you calling in the night. I will go Lord, if you lead me.

I will hold your people in my heart…"

After being ceremonially robed in white and celebrated with hugs and flowers, I realized that I was a miracle standing within myself: a servant of God and a steward of peace and love. And I was home in it all! As my dear friend sang and the tears streamed down my face, I recalled a vision that I had had while in meditation only weeks before. Crystal-clear within my mind's eye Christ appeared behind me, and pouring the chalice of wine over me as I knelt in a white flowing robe. I experienced this physically, as a warm sensation, embraced as he called me to be his own, a witness for him in the world.

CHAPTER 5

The Miracle Parish

After the ordination I was given my first parish, St. Peter's by the Sea, not knowing I was sent there to close it. It was drowning and there were only a handful of parishioners left, as the others had already scattered to different churches. So, there we stood, a motley band of saints and sinners, but we stood… and carried the cross we bore, determined not to be buried at the bottom of the ocean without a fight. We leaned on the energies of all who had passed through those Episcopal red doors before us… and then came our miracle.

St Peter's was saved only a few Sundays after I got there. Saved by a sweet and desperate Liberian mother who had the courage to step out of her pew in the middle of a Sunday service. Falling to her knees in the center of the church aisle, face in hands, she sobbed for help. She struggled to speak about her three teen boys who were, at that moment, on the run being pursued by thugs who had just overthrown their government. These thugs were rounding up government officials and their families for execution. It was a brutal regime and the boys were on their own, knowing to run only when night skies darkened the horizon. Their father was out of the country on government work and couldn't get back to them. They were alone and terrified of being gunned down.

So, here we were, a pathetic number rushing to assist her. I flew from behind the altar. I knelt beside her as the 15 or so others circled around her, lifting her up embracing her and without words, easing her into our hearts never to let her go.

The first thing we decided to do was to gather all the names of the people throughout all the years, that had ever attended the church. We wrote them for a donation and graciously most all responded. The bishop matched their response and that's when the miracle of 15 became 80, much like in the Bible story about the loaves and fishes. Our sweet, kind mama went to Liberia not knowing where her boys were, the equivalent to trying to find a needle in a haystack. To everyone's surprise, she actually found them hiding in Sierra Leone! Of course, we shouldn't have been surprised at anything in this saga, as looking back it was all orchestrated from that beautiful woman's spirit.

I can hardly describe that sacred moment when they returned. We all gathered to welcome them home. And not unlike the parable of the loaves and fishes, we were fed then and for years to come, by the sacred heart of a mother's cry.

From that moment forward the church grew and wasn't hurled into the sea. Rather, St. Peter's began to walk on water, reaching out to stranded seafarers, looking for a safe harbor to find their God. St. Peter's by-the-Sea became known as the miracle parish in the diocese. Many have asked me through the years, how I grew this dying parish. I just simply begin: "Once upon a Sunday Service…"

After serving this parish for over seven years, upon coming out as a lesbian and initiating a divorce from my husband of 30 years, I was asked to leave St. Peter's-by-the Sea. I still can't describe in words the pain I felt for my church as they were told by the bishop that I had to leave them. Such deep heart-felt pride I had for them, as they strongly stood up in church and responded; "You can't take her from us. She has taught us about unconditional love and we want to give that back to her now."

We are told, when we are ordained, that we are the spiritual mothers and fathers of our churches. The day I heard that plea, I felt like our kind Liberian mama, as my heart broke open with a mother's cry. "I will continue to hold you. To hold you all, in the womb of my soul."

CHAPTER 6

The Voice That Could Never Be Dismissed

Upon coming out, leaving my husband and children and both my physical and spiritual homes, I thought, "How could I do this?" So much inside me screamed to go back. I always knew all my life that voice that could never be dismissed. When I was called forward there was no turning back for me.

I could not deny my love for Kaye nor the hypocrisy of the church. Kaye was a woman that I had been introduced to by a friend, during a spiritual workshop. We recognized each other upon first meeting and it was love at first sight.

And so, I began my journey to another God not knowing where it would lead me. I wanted to find a church that welcomed us and a place where we felt normal in our love as I had with my husband; not afraid to hold hands, hug or sit close to each other. I was led to the Metropolitan Community Church (MCC) for the LGBTQ+ community it offered. And I felt at home there with my partner. I talked with the minister about my life and he and I developed a close collegial bond. He helped me with my grief, especially with my adult children. It was so devastating for them and our relationship was suffering under the weight of this break in our family. I was not only grieving for myself. I was also holding my husband's grief in my heart, as well as my children's, not knowing how it could or would ever end. My nights were literally spent torn in two. First, with a love I never knew was possible. Secondly, with a grief and a guilt I never knew was bearable. All compounded with conflicting thoughts of going back or staying. I cried almost every night as Kaye held me.

I try to stop the bleeding of my heart

My feeble efforts take part, but not enough to stop yet a dribble or a cry.

How long can this go on before a heart must die.

For several weeks and months, when my friends would ask me, what did it feel like to all of a sudden realize I was gay after all those years of marriage.

First, I told them it wasn't all of a sudden. It had been creeping in for many a year in all sorts of different ways, mostly under my conscious radar. Second, the only way I could explain it to them was through the intimacy aspect, as all else was pretty much the same dailyness of living we all participate in.

To help them understand, I would liken it to watching an old black and white film of a beautiful sexy love scene of a heterosexual couple, enchanted with each other. They could experience the feelings they would have while watching and where it would carry them away to. Then, take that same movie with a gay couple with all those feelings and put it in cinematic 3D technicolor, and that's the difference for me. That's the wow factor! I believe everyone I explained it to in that fashion could understand the change in the level of passion and intimacy it gave me. I guess that was true, as I found I didn't have to answer more questions, thank goodness, on that subject at least.

Several months later the minister at the Metropolitan Community Church called me stating he had to go back to Colorado. And that He had put my name in as Interim Minister with other names that were applying for that position. I thanked him for his faith in me and being so kind, knowing that I didn't have a chance. When he had asked me to preach in the church, the people would say they loved my sermons, but also knew what a baby lesbian I was, and we all would laugh. How could I possibly lead a LGBTQ+ church? No, I was certain this was way out of my league and I wasn't gay enough. So of course, I put it out of my mind.

A couple of weeks later I received a call from the church nominating committee asking me to come in for an interview. I knew it was their policy to interview all the candidates so I wasn't surprised about the call. The call that came next and gave me the one-two punch that knocked me out was, "Reverend, we have deliberated for a while and we are calling you as our Interim Minister." My immediate thought was, are they insane? And, who is this other God I was journeying towards?

And of course, my questions began as always. What do I need to do for my next step?

How do I prepare? Read, study, be still, reflect? And then I heard:

> ***"Just look for me. I will be there as you've never seen me before.***
>
> ***Do not fear as there are angels and guides all around you.***
>
> ***You will know what to do.***
>
> ***Stay the road, they will guide you.***
>
> ***Look for them in the wisdom of others, in the books you pick up, in the seeds you scatter and in the hearts you hear speak."***

Will it be soon?

> ***"Now! It is here and it is now. Drop all - Come."***

Who are you now? Are you the God I've known in the past?

"Are you the Patricia I've known in the past?" No.

"Then...no."

But aren't you the same now, forever and always?

"Are you the same now, forever and always?" No.

"Then...no."

So, are you saying, as I change, you change?

"Yes, I change to allow you to grow in me and as you grow,

I love you into newness, re-births, and re-awakenings.

Your divinity stretches within you and your divine self gets to look more and more like me.

All sorts of mysteries open up to you as well as false doctrines and inherent beliefs.

You step forward and you go on..."

But I'm having trouble naming you now. Why is that?

"I've become larger. You are in a place of transition and I, as well as you must wait

for what you will call me, or what you will not call me."

I'm so confused. I thought I was a Christian all my life and now…now I'm not sure what I am. Do you know what I am?

"Ah, yes my Patricia, you are my dreams taken flesh.

You are the compassionate heart of a woman.

I have allowed you your pain so your heart could break open and find its way out - it's way home to me again.

I know you can understand what I am saying, even though your pain is still with you.

You cannot marry Divinity without the heights of Ecstasy and the lows of Agony; and remember, you are not alone."

I know to give it all up to you. I try, I try to let it go.

"I know you are willing."

So, will my heart ever be at rest?

…Never mind, I know!

CHAPTER 7

Holding My Breath

Ministry in the Metropolitan Community Church could only be explained as a remedial education in the LGBTQ+ community. It was a tradition that the minister be invited by every household to dinner with their partner. This immersed me into a cultural overload that I can only say left me stumbling, while loving every moment of my new lesbian life. I didn't have to question who I was to myself any longer, nor have that deep hole in the pit of my stomach that ached with a mystery unknown. I had a home base now and yearned to know and name my new God.

Now, this didn't take all my awkwardness away as their minister. I prayed every night for God to take it slow. I knew so little about this new culture of mine, with all its different customs, art, music, social groups and history. I started doubting myself, asking how I was to be their spiritual leader and guide. I sat in my office voraciously reading the church's mission, purpose and goals. And how to perform a celebration for the blessing of same sex unions to name just a few, as I wanted to be prepared for anything. Well, the joke was on me.

The third Sunday I was there, setting up for our service, a man came out of his pew and asked if he could talk with me for just a moment. He began by saying he was in the process of, "changing from a man to a woman" but had only one dilemma. His wife wanted to stay with him as he did with her, but she had one request - that he keep his penis. He asked me what he should do. The first thought in my swirling mind was, "Ok, God if this is taking it slow, we're in a lot of trouble. I surely need some help here!" I immediately said, "I hear you and it is a question that needs much thought and consideration. It can't be taken up when we have but moments before our service begins. Come to me after the service and we'll make an appointment.

Now, to understand how surprising and awkward this was for me as a minister, I need you to understand in all my many years as a spiritual mother of a church, I was never approached with many sexual problems. The heterosexual community would be too embarrassed to bring that to their priest, and I would be too embarrassed to take that subject up with them. Being only in the heterosexual white middle class world all my life, surely didn't prepare me for any of this… So, I had only hoped that the flush I felt in my cheeks didn't give me away to this beautiful spirit.

A few weeks later a lesbian couple came into the office to ask for a blessing of their union (this was a time even before civil unions). They sat next to each other, looking lovingly at each other. One of the women finally said, "Go ahead and tell her, it's our minister and you can trust her."

She proceeded to tell me she was 'trans' and she had been a Roman Catholic Priest. Without a change in demeanor, I looked at her with a nod of acceptance as I felt myself slide under the desk. It was profound in how that moment was imprinted on my mind. She was defrocked and banned from the church, and her family had never spoken to her since. My mind now went back to the taking it slow talk with God. We talked about being colleagues and during the following year she was so helpful and supportive of me. Subsequently, before I was to take my leave from the church, she took me aside and laughingly said to me that she had something to tell me before I left. She said she had seen me "slide under my desk" as I was so fervently trying not to reveal my surprise when she told me who she was. Those were her exact words, the same ones marked so indelibly on my mind the year before. I was embarrassed for that split second until we both smiled and hugged knowing we had come a long way and would miss each other. These were just a few of my encounters with the shame and pain of the LGBTQ+ community. I realized, as a wounded healer, that I would be addressing these traumas that so plagued me and this community, my community, for the rest of my life.

From that time on, I would hold my breath before anyone came into my office to ask advice or simply to be heard. Having become aware that I was actually there to learn from them, as I realized that all the reading in the cosmos couldn't prepare me. Only the conquering of my own homophobic fears and woundedness, could elevate my abilities to serve this community.

CHAPTER 8
Parallel Positions

After the typical one year of interim service at the Metropolitan Community Church my time there came to an end. I was home, sitting on my bed reading and the phone rang. I saw it was the newly elected Bishop who, in his position of Suffragan (assistant) Bishop had once told me I would never lose my parish, on account of being a lesbian. But I also had concern about what would happen should he ever find out that I had previously ministered at the Metropolitan Community Church. A church of a different doctrine. I froze, not wanting to pick it up, fearful of what he had to say to me. I certainly knew I could be defrocked, never to be an Episcopal priest again. I finally picked up the phone shaking, wondering if he knew where I had been.

Immediately, the short conversation began. "Pat, I know where you have been and I want you to come home now." Filled with overwhelming shock and amazement, I could not speak. The next thing I heard was, "Pat are you there?" "Yes, thank you!"

finally broke through my tears. All I could remember from the rest of our conversation was, "My secretary will call you with a date to come in, so we can find an interim position to get you started at a church near you." After I hung up, my mind buckled under the strain with my knees to follow. Kneeling, I caught my breath and I asked myself, "What the hell just happened?"

After a year of an interim ministry position, I found myself once again as a priest-incharge of a lovely small Church in New England that needed much love and growth. At this same time the church was facing a schism over sexuality which came dragging on the robes of our newly elected Bishop of New Hampshire. Gene Robinson was an openly gay priest in a committed relationship. The media was all over this news. Gay episcopal priests everywhere had to decide now what their responsibility was, and if they wanted to expose themselves. Many lesbian and gay priests that had previously feared to come out, were now willing to step up and form groups committed to having their voices heard. During our Diocesan Convention that year, we each took a turn at the pulpit proclaiming our sexuality and our rights to serve.

Well, you could probably guess what a dialogue we created. You could literally see the anger rise up, like black smoke in our cathedral, as the divide started to take on its momentum.

The Bible was their first line of defense and so yet again another great debate began. Bloody words and violent rhetoric spewed, spitting on the flames of love that continues, even to this day, to change the message of Christ.

Unlike many of my colleagues I was inundated with newspaper reporters and people in our parishes with questions and concerns. In one newspaper article, displaying a large picture of myself, you could read:

"The Rev. Patricia Gallagher, the openly gay rector of St. James Episcopal Church, supports proposals at the General Convention to formally endorse ordination of homosexuals, and to create a same sex union liturgy. But she concedes the heated debate has already caused a schism within the church."

Some months later, this article and my activism caused a schism in my church and I was asked to leave. As I took my leave, I realized again that there are no coincidences in life. The Metropolitan Community Church was put in my path to educate and allow me to walk my walk and to talk my talk. To be willing and able to stand in my courage, helping to heal the gaps between the gay and straight communities in our church. Those two worlds collided, fought and reconciled within me during my ministry at MCC. And so, I could empathize with the pain of others, having just gone through this struggle before them.

During the next few years, I was invited to become priest-in-charge of St Mark's parish. I was also asked to be on committees, and speak and write letters, to help bridge the gap between the homosexual and heterosexual aligned parishes. Sometimes reaching the stars and other times reaching my limits. The bishop tried so hard to hear and please both sides that neither side was happy with him. He feared a schism would run rampant in his diocese and he would not be able to negotiate with either side. I would talk to him about sitting on the fence and that he needed to jump off one way or another, as this was killing him and any forward motion from either side of the aisle. In the times I thought I would be finished, burnt-out with this oppressive work, humanity showed its face in the strangest of ways.

For example:

The bishop had organized a meeting for conservative and liberal clergy on the issue of, does God say it's ok to be gay. Funny way of putting it. It would be a lawyer's good fortune to argue this "he-says, she-says" case. I was asked to attend, as the lesbian priest.

We sat in a circle behind tables, and as I scanned the room, I wasn't surprised at the hostel energy rising up in certain quadrants. I was sitting there, with only one other gay priest who had been "out" in the church for years. The rules were set and we began. It was a peaceful conversation in words, but the tone set a vibe of disdain and shame, which I felt landing upon me. There I was, the only female in the room with the "old boys' network", as we called it. I was used to being in the minority as a female priest. Now, however, I felt it twice over as the representative lesbian priest. But then a strange thing happened. As I listened, I actually heard them, and my heart broke open as the Christ in them diminished before my eyes. I could see their conflict and struggles to reconcile the basic Christian message of unconditional love. I spoke last and told my story of coming out to the bishop, my church and my gut wrenching talks with my husband of thirty years and my children. I allowed myself to be vulnerable even if I was to be eaten alive.

After the meeting as we were all gathering and talking in different groups, I was touched on my shoulder by a priest I knew from the anti-gay conservative group. I turned as he began, "I just want to apologize for anything I said that could have hurt you. Please don't take it personally. A group of us have been talking and we would like to pray with you". I hesitated with thoughts running through my head a hundred miles an hour. Are they going to pray to save me, or pray to hate the sin but love the sinner, or worse to see my immoral ways and pray for me to change? I literally took a step back to look him in the eyes to respond with a "NO". Instead to my utter surprise I nodded a yes, and with their arms around one another they formed a circle around me. I bowed my head in complete submission as they started to pray. Calmness captured my being as I rested in myself, feeling I could love them no matter how they prayed. I believe, at that precise moment, we all felt the same magical spell of love that transcends all else, and we found ourselves lost in one another's souls... at least for a few seconds in time. They prayed for my journey and my partner, and that God bless me in all things for the future. We left one another with hugs and a respect none of us could have ever seen coming.

The tragedy of this gathering was that never was this group summoned back to continue the softening that had occurred, to strengthen the potential for change that was on the horizon of our hearts. As time went on, we could feel this happening time and time again, taking one step forward, then one step back.

CHAPTER 9

A Goodbye Letter

Dear Friends,

I will never forget our raised joy-filled voices singing Hallelujah during my years of ministry here at St. Mark's church.

I will never forget meeting with the vestry (Board of the Church) for the first time with strained looks and vague smiles. But also, with hearts streaming with hope and love to find a way to survive, as the church was close to closing, and actually having to be sold.

I will never forget your impassioned request for me to become your priest after that initial interview. How you broke conventional protocol with your quick decision, turning to the diocesan consultant asking what the next step was. She replied, "Well, before we go to the bishop with this, you and Reverend Pat will need to take the time to go home, pray on it and decide what to do".

A woman sitting across from me immediately blurted out "How long does it take you to pray"? I immediately blurted back, "Not too long, as I already prayed and that's why I'm here."

The vestry members took a silent look around at each other and then hired me on the spot! The look on the consultant's face was not to be missed as she stumbled to say, "Well, we have to meet protocol and I don't know of a time that an immediate decision like this has ever been made in the past".

I knew this consultant well, and she was considered the best consultant in the diocese. Most everyone loved her approach to things and the kindness and concern that she had for the people in her care. As this meeting was coming to an end, I believe that I was the only one to recognize the twinkle in her eyes expressing her thoughts. You go ladies and gentlemen. You made the right choice, and I'll make sure we get this done.

It was incredible, and surely an unconventional first meeting, as were all of my first meetings with each of you. I was touched by your unwavering faith. I have truly never experienced a church community like St. Mark's and I am sad that I must take my leave now. I am forever grateful for the lives that touched mine, allowing us to be one with God and each other. This church will survive here with the soup kitchen. The building isn't the church. You are the church and a finer and more gracefilled church would be hard to find anywhere. So, remember, Don't Worry - Be Happy!!!! And know you are a people with heart and soul that will carry you anywhere you wish to go.

So… happy journeying. And please keep me in your hearts, as I will keep you always, in mine.

George Elliot once wrote:

"Only in the agony of parting do we look into the depths of love".

I have a depth of love and gratitude for you all that fills me with a joy that will always be in my reach. Thank you.

Blessings and peace,
Reverend Pat

The bishop's reply to my letter sent me to a place of extreme sadness, as I knew it was my final goodbye.

Dear Pat,

When I returned from sabbatical, I read your letter of May 28th about your plans to leave St Mark's Church.

Your decision comes as a surprise and I must say at the outset, how much I and the diocese will miss your presence and ministry. You have been a prophet for the breadth of God's love among us. You have served so creatively and faithfully St. Mark's Church during this time of enormous transition for that parish. I understand that the process is well underway for the sale of the church property to the soup kitchen, and the new status of the congregation allowing them to stay and worship in its' historic building. I think there could not have been a more creative or substantial blessing for the parish than the direction in which you and they have moved.

Pat, I shall miss you among us for sure. I will always treasure the time we had together at your spiritual life center and in the many churches you served. We have seen one another through some difficult times and grappled with significant concerns and issues. I pray every blessing upon you as you go forward to a new Chapter in your life, and I would love to know more about your plans. Every blessing be with you, and again thank you for being you and a vessel of God's love.

Yours in Christ,
Bishop

This was the last church I served as a parish priest and the last time I saw the man who held me with tears in his eyes, as I told him Kaye had left me for another. Even with all the tension and differences we had regarding the questionings of homosexuality in the church, this beautiful spirit of a man, looked at me in horror when I told him Kaye had left me after ten years. I could see the shock come over him and the heads turning to look, as he spoke with a loud voice that could be heard by many in that meeting room. "Oh, Shit! No Pat, no Pat!" as he pulled me into his arms. How holy it felt when he held me.

Assuredly, this was a man with a divine presence and I shall miss him!

CHAPTER 10

What the Hell!

During the same period of time that I was at St. Mark's, I was also running a spiritual life center with my partner Kaye. This spiritual life center gave me my heart back after just having come out as a lesbian. I was feeling lost in the ecstasy of discovering my true self and in the agony of what I was losing. I was the first to find sanctuary in this place. Chuck Shepard literally handed me the keys to a house that he had built with his son. It boasted two large open green fields and a pond on a pristine parcel of 40 acres, in what seemed an ideal land for inspiration and visions. His only request: "Do something for the glory of God on this land!" And for one dollar and a promise I held the deed. I made that promise to Chuck with the purest of intentions, but it was also a promise I made to God deep within my soul.

Our mission statement was "to create, hold and promote an awareness of sacred space where deep transformation can occur, and to offer a supportive environment where those who come can find peace and common ground".

This is where I fell in love with a universal God. For the first time. I looked deep inside myself and asked, what erroneous beliefs operate in my life? And a flood of answers came fast and furiously!

Christian teachings stating that Jesus Christ is the only way to eternal life.

Christian judgement that some people are more worthy than others.

The Bible is the only word of God

(And this is the one that sucked the faith in the church right out of me!)

If you don't believe "all of the above" you will go to hell.

What the Hell!!!

It brought me back to being taught these truths as a young child in a parochial grammar school. And a feeling that my mother was going to hell, because she was Jewish and did not believe in Jesus Christ. Well, you can imagine how a little girl of eleven would internalize that. But hell no, not me!

I defended my mother stating she was the most loving and giving person. Just meeting her anyone would know she would go straight to heaven. I proceeded to argue. Even at eleven years old asking, "what about the people in other countries that we had been studying about who hadn't even heard of Jesus? Would they go to hell too?" Upon writing this, I now understand that is why and how my pilgrimage began. I was fighting to know who my God of love really was, and is.

A crazed sickness runs through all Christian religions polluting the essence of Christianity. From crusades to witch hunts, inquisitions, prejudice and oppression… from privileged hierarchies, men abusing power, women treated as second class and discriminated against… to sexual abuse with no consequences, and on and on and on, even to the present day.

My judgements were harsh and stuck in the throat of my being. Confident in my assessment of the contradictions of the core of Christian beliefs, I wanted resolution. And so, I looked elsewhere for spiritual wisdom. I yearned for a true spiritual life and wanted to heal this place of pain and struggle within me.

CHAPTER 11

Sanctuary/My Sanctuary

Dear Chuck,

Jay told me he talked with you last week. He felt very awkward because he didn't know how to tell you about our situation. I should have written to you sooner, but have been in such a transition I haven't gotten to everyone as yet. Jay and I have separated and will be divorced within the next few months. Our separation did not come about because of a lack of love between us or any nastiness. I had to leave because I've finally admitted that I am gay. Once I came out to myself there was nowhere else to go but out of a heterosexual marriage. This has been a horrific time of change, not the least of which is the pain this has caused Jay. I'm living in Chester now with my partner Kaye, all that much closer to the Sanctuary.

As it turns out this became my sanctuary first. I moved there when I first left Jay before coming to Chester. I've done a lot of soul searching these last months. I have had the strong sense that perhaps the Sanctuary should also have a specialized ministry to the LGBTQ+ community. Still a retreat center, still a quiet place for prayer, meditation, peace and healing, with the same offering to the gay community as well. A group underserved and for the most part, desperately in need of permission to find a loving and accepting God.

The way I describe my journey, is that when I went deeply enough inside to find God, I found myself - the core self - the person I truly am. And I heard, "It is good!" I believe what I recently read, that eighty percent of the spiritual journey is about self-acceptance. I think I might even go further saying, perhaps all of it. And so here I am!

At this point, I've found a new group of people ready and willing to work with me, form a board and write an amended mission statement. These women and men are therapists, engineers, nurses, healers, fund raisers, clergy, straight, gay and lesbian. Funny how, when one is in the right place with oneself, the universe comes to meet them.

Please give my love to your wife. I hope all is well with you both and I hope to hear from you soon.

Love,
Pat

And so, the happenings began. Kaye and I moved into the house that Chuck built with his son. The hives were filled with bees. Volunteers cut and chopped back the underbrush, repaired stone walls and worked on an 80-foot labyrinth. Individuals and churches supported us and all would be coming on a regular basis to help us put up a "yurt." Whatever that was!? One church awarded us a grant to buy a round, canvas building that provided space for meetings, workshops, conversations, meditations, celebrations and worship… ah, a Yurt!!

We set it up in the field, not far from the house, with a circular wooden deck around its 30-foot diameter. This took precision cuts and the tireless workings of our genius engineer. Inside, there was a beautiful wooden floor partially covered by a lovely oriental rug for warmth, comfortable furniture for informal conversations and a moveable table/altar. A wood pellet-burning stove finished off the room with a few minor final touches. The rumored, initial homophobia of a lesbian couple moving in gave way to friendships over the course of just a few months, and we settled in for years of congeniality and growth.

The townspeople supported us at planning and zoning meetings, one of which was to declare a local dirt road which bordered the Sanctuary's property, a scenic road. Our neighbors would say, as they stepped onto the property, that they could actually feel the loving energy. They would come by with cuttings for our gardens, hay our field, and bring eggs from their chickens, to be part of the expansion of the love that was enveloping their neighborhood. So many hands, hearts, heads, prayers, and surely no one would be surprised if I said miracles, greeted us each day as we prepared our physical, mental and spiritual bodies for the ride of a lifetime.

One of our many offerings was a course we named, "Tomorrow's God." This was developed after reading Neale Donald Walsh's "Conversations with God", as well as books on quantum physics, metaphysics, existentialism and consciousness awakening.

We were also influenced by movies like "What the Bleep Do We Know" and "The Secret". The course entailed readings, role plays, movie-watching, and journaling. The journaling notebooks given out, contained questions to ponder and be considered while writing for the next session's discussions.

Questions like:

What does spirituality mean to you?

What are the dogmas in your life?

How do these dogmas govern how you perceive yourself?

If thoughts can affect the molecular structure of water, what are your thoughts doing to your reality?

How do thoughts, yours and others affect your spirituality?

How has the religious paradigm that you grew up with, or even live with today, affected your perception of reality in a positive or negative sense - or both?

Identify some current paradigms in your life that you desire to change.

Why do you wish to change? What do you think the outcome of this change will mean for you and your spirituality - your family and friends - your community - the world at large?

This is where a new journey began, unlike any I had before. It would take me within the spaces of my mind, heart and soul, flipping me upside down with new and incredible unknown worlds of possibilities opening within me. During this time, I felt something come at me gently and explode its energy within and around me. My body felt awakened, buzzing, calling me to rise from its shallow slumber. I could hear voices lower than my own speak to me:

"We are here with you. Stay and feel our presence.

We know you have questions that we will answer for you in time.

The time has come for you to feel your inheritance.

Now rest as we rest in you."

CHAPTER 12

A Screaming Cry of a Motherless Woman

I need to digress a bit in my timeline to explain how the next journey began. When I was about thirty, my father called to inform me that my mother was sick, and they were taking her to the hospital for breathing treatments and tests. Her doctor said she had pneumonia. My mother was the person I loved with the deepest passion. Except for my young children, no one else came close to that quality of love, and to this day never has. We were so close we would finish each other's sentences, similar to twins knowing each other's movements and thoughts. Looking back, I realize that we must have been in some kind of a loving relationship in a past life. So, you can be certain that I was present with her in that hospital, just minutes after the call. As I walked in, I found my father and brother sitting with her in the room, talking and laughing with her about some silly thing. I felt in my gut that something was very wrong but laughed and engaged with them, nonetheless. Orderlies soon arrived to take my mother for tests and lung x-rays. We sat, waiting.

The same routine followed the next day, with additional blood work and tests. Just outside her room, my father met me with a wave of energy that nearly collapsed me to the floor. I was overtaken by his tangible fear and grief. He then, released the news: my mother had lung cancer! Small Cell Carcinoma Lung Cancer, one of the fastest growing and deadly forms of lung cancer. It had already metastasized to her liver and she had roughly three months to live. All that could be done for her now was a few radiation treatments to ease her pain and support her breathing. My father was given a phone number to initiate hospice services. He went on to inform me that I had to break the news to my mother, as neither he nor my brother knew how to. They would give me all the time I needed alone, to inform her of her demise. This I heard through an unfamiliar hazelike veil, shocked and numb with terror. Like this was all happening somewhere far-off, in a distant reality. I just stared at him, nodding robotically and then walked quietly, obediently, into my mother's room. Sitting down on her bed, I took her hand. My eyes met hers and not knowing where to begin, I was speechless. She was the one who then said, "It's alright. You can tell me all the details. I see you. I feel your pain and know, looking at you now, that there will not be a good outcome."

This is when I truly discovered the significance of hospice and where my grief began. Losing my mother incrementally, over a three-month period, instilled a deep grief that seemed to hijack my spirit. It put me in a strange land where I didn't know the language and the oxygen levels were so low, I had trouble breathing. I was not only emotionally depleted, but also physically challenged, as her primary caregiver. At times, I too was physically ill. The help of my husband, and the love I saw displayed by my sweet young children as they huddled around their beloved grandmother, allowed me to continue on. They played near her, sang her songs, and gifted her with endless pieces of crayoned art work. Yet, I existed in a dark hole of grief, where no one's reach could touch or lift me.

However, there was Hospice. Hospice carried me through this time and let me know my feelings were okay to speak about, openly. They provided my children with a social worker who shared magical story times, allowing their innocent minds an outlet to talk about the pieces that didn't seem to fit when looking at their grandmother. I couldn't begin to show these dedicated care givers my gratitude, but knew somewhere in the near future I would be one of them.

I had never known such gut-wrenching grief before, nor felt such intense emotions. The screaming cry of a young mother becoming motherless was beyond my ability to express and would be held within me forever, it seemed. I also felt at times, momentary relief, the kind that we can experience during our darkest moments. It's that sliver of hope that pierces our being, radiating light within, exposing the truth for an instant. The truth is that we are embraced always in unconditional love and healing grace. Such a moment occurred in a meditation for me. Envisioning my death, I saw my mother come to meet me on the other side, as she took my hand to lead me across.

Two years later, I applied for the chaplaincy position at the same hospice that had so lovingly and respectfully cared for my mother, as well as my family. Here, my love affair with hospice continued. Even after retiring from priestly parish work many years later, I would continue to work within hospice programs as a chaplain and bereavement coordinator. I became present to both the euphoria and agony that accompanies a life released and the grieving of those left behind, searching to find a way to walk without them.

Eight years later, fully immersed in the ministry of death and dying, I felt a calling to serve differently. I realized that I was rounding a corner as I did many years ago when I chose to retire from parish work, though I still was unaware of what this new way of serving would look like. Nevertheless, it was clear to me that I was meant to retire from Hospice at this time. Again, I grieved at leaving so many behind. This felt like a type of existential grief, realizing that I was approaching the end years of my life. I prayed for the courage to find a new way to serve; to continue singing my song authentically, but with a new twist:

Here I am Lord, God/Goddess

Is it I? I have heard you calling in the night.

I will go, if you need me

I will hold your people in my heart…

This grief was an anxious grief, consuming me. I was vulnerable to the fear of the unknown which was eating at my soul. I had to again ponder what my purpose was. I didn't want it said on my deathbed that I hadn't played the music within me. I had heard that when you are born, the song is in your heart and it stays there until you sing it. I don't want to die with that music still in me. As a seeker of truth I want my song to be heard, always looking for the godly connections and the oneness in all and everything. Maybe that's what a mystic looks like.

I need not be afraid of seeing faith and morality through different lenses. I can witness things beyond this world's conventional view of reality, while also being empathetic to the many belief systems inherent within the tenets held by the authority of many churches. I realized that if I stayed within the walls of any one dogma, the pain and eventual spiritual death that I'd seen a multitude of times in others would kill my spirit as well.

Freed-up now to go a bit unconventional, there I stood with a clever grin. So mischievously, I began to play in the halls of the spiritualist churches and as before, heard, "It is good!" I felt a cleansing, a sense of universal clearing, absorbing me into the divine oneness of the universe.

And then, out of the blue, in crept the same funny God as the one that had crept in at the Metropolitan Community Church. I was asked to be the interim minister now of a spiritualist church. I immediately thought, "Here we go again, into the school of hard knocks", as I laughed myself to sleep that night.

I started-out on this new leg of my journey taking courses to become a spiritualist, followed by a very informal process to become an ordained interim minister. There I was, with my head in books again, studying for hours at a time while going to psychic development courses. We covered subjects regarding clairvoyance, clairaudience, telepathy, channeling, mediumship, astral projection, and the nature of empaths, intuitives and the like.

This merry-go-round went round and round as my mystical experiences turned into something that I could relate to, but differently. I realized that the word mystic could easily be a synonym for clairaudient, for example. I ate it all up like cake, and the sweetness gave my mind hallucinations, as I started to realize that I had been channeling through writing all along. Previously, I had held fears around the concept of the paranormal and never dreamed that that was something to overcome. But now, like homosexuality, I rather soared to greet it.

Looking back on this time in my life, I can see, without a doubt, why I had always been drawn toward psychic activity, but afraid to go there. I was brought here now, to understand more deeply, lessons from the other side. To know and understand my spirit guides, and to finally be awakened to the intricacies of my journey.

"Wow!", I thought. "I guess I can die now. What more could there be?" And of course, again little did I know new challenges and growing opportunities were brewing, in the form of a pandemic.

PART II
AWAKENING

CHAPTER 13

Universal Cracking In Us All

Covid was beginning to take over the world as I was taking my leave from the spiritualist temple. The quarantine sinks in, as I look out my window glued to the chair at my desk, yawning into the sleepiness of winter and everything stopping outside. Pulling my sweatshirt over my head, chilled from the weather and this great paradigm shift, I began to hear a question start pounding in my mind.

"Who am I, here now?"

I am inconsistent with this world. As it now spins into chaos, I'm experiencing a greater sense of calm. I see the world in a merging spectrum of transparent colors rather than in the contrasts of reds, yellows, blues, blacks and whites. I see it as a whole rather than its parts. I sense the sun, even behind the clouds, and I want…

I want to feel the true essence of love, as well as give it.

I want to touch the wisdom of my age.

I want to immerse myself in all things beautiful.

I want to kiss the ground I walk on and sense the happiness of creation.

I want to breathe easily as I encounter the shadows of death.

I want to surrender to all the God's I've known with a tenacious gratitude.

I want to realize more fully the I Am God within, united with love unconditional.

I want to know that we are here for the glory of being. Just being.

I want the right to hold each other's hearts in the flowering of our souls.

I've heard it said that the mystical quest is the re-telling of the universe's need to seek experience and the individual's need to find the sacred.

"Where will I go on this timely quest? This time, to the woodlands I will seek, for to tell me where to plant my feet. Tracking my scent as I go within, finding the light, that soon goes dim.

My soul stretches until I reach the center core where light and energy are no more, and everything turns into nothingness as I proceed to explain or entertain… the void. The void where we become the eternal beginning and end of the universal seed.

Shifting back to the material reality of this pandemic, I tried to wrap my mind around all the information coming out about covid. This took mental and spiritual discipline. I found refuge in the new silence of our world. It became a gift and meditation my comfort. All that I wanted to do was write and listen to the voice of my soul, maintain balance amongst this new craziness and pay off my karmic debts. Stepping outside, I could see that the world was reforming in fresh colors, freedoms and sounds. With each breath I wanted to experience the world through these new perspectives blossoming in my mind. I wanted to understand it's physics, the geography of my heart and the mathematics of the universe.

During this time, about twelve of us formed a spiritual group.

Our mission statement read:

"To come together in a quiet sacred space, for our mutual support, spiritual expression, and to learn and to evolve."

Our goal read:

"To create a place of acceptance and mutual respect for self-discovery and inner growth."

Our group dwindled down to six in response to the mask mandates and the general fear of covid, although we continued to meet in different homes distancing ourselves. We meditated and prayed for healing of the world and for each other. It was a journey that none of us foresaw. I believe it allowed us to not only survive the quarantine but actually grow through it. Like so many the internet became our lifeline. I found myself meditating for hours at a time and channeling through writing. So, I asked. "What is the message of this pandemic and quarantine?" And I was told:

> *"There is no message, the cycle of time and space has been converging and the residue left now is being swept away.*
>
> *The winds will be steady and fierce and all will know we are in an evolution.*
>
> *No need for fear, for the elements are in place and the beings are aligned to help.*
>
> *You need to stop and quiet down to see the unfolding of the happenings on Earth.*
>
> *You need to stop and quiet down to hear the sounds, that make your Earth unintelligible and unreal.*
>
> *We are here to lift you up, all beings, out of this illusion and show you the Earth is safe and sustainable; and remind you*

of the sacred symbols we have given you throughout time to heal your planet.

Take this time to rest in your quarantine, in order to accept the grace given for a new humanity, yearning to burst forth to fill the Earth with more than fear, rather with vibrations that bring in harmony and peace.

We are here to help you understand and take it forward.

Be still and listen - be still and listen and move with us.

All is well."

CHAPTER 14

Mother Earth Answers Our Longings

The next day I received yet another channeling about the quarantine, thus adding to my many gods - a mother goddess:

"Take it for what it is.

It is the U (you) effect.

What one does, ripples.

What one doesn't do, stills.

The U effect is guided by U whether positive or negative, moving or stagnant.

The world has come to a halt.

The silence left deafens U to hear the Earth moaning, asking U to re-connect."

I believe we have putrefied the Earth into something that's becoming unrecognizable. We must gentle its wrath. It is screaming with hunger and retching from thirst. We must soothe its existence, the monstrous shapes that are forming from explosive fires to hideous shadows of prejudice and wars, earthquakes, tornados and landslides. These are all of what lies inside each one of us.

We must take control of our egos and give compassion back to our planet. One by one we must feed inside ourselves what the Earth needs to feed on, trusting again in our nurturing awareness to balance the energies in and outside of ourselves.

I can feel the Earth moving heavily within me, just as I feel that the few are many now and the many are mounting. The Earth is humming with anticipated new beginnings, buzzing with great possibilities as we free fall into a new dimension of love without judgement, wisdom without words, and willingness without limitations. We have come to a place where we can express patterns of expansive awareness of co-creating as one, in the swirling of universal energy. It's here for all for any, that want to be released from the shadows of chaos and soar to new heights. Aware of what is to come, what is possible, as the new collective observes itself with greater depth and sensitivity.

Our spiritual gatherings still continue to this day. We have been meeting for some time now. Finding ourselves in each other, touching what is the other to find what is in each of us, trying to promote good intentions, fighting our judgements to release only compassion and love. As we six continue to expand, more understanding and new energies are pressing forward within us. Realizing it is time to make new commitments. We, and the world turn to look within itself to shape the structure of an evolution of higher dimensional realities. And I was being told:

> ***"You cannot be in a world of make believe sitting in the mud of your mind, trying to find happiness. This world of illusions will not and cannot satisfy. Step out into the expansion of time and space and see all the possibilities.***
>
> ***Awaiting for you is unity marked by evolutionary proportions entering into new worlds, new beginnings, new dimensions of consciousness and desire.***
>
> ***This road leads to intergalactic adventures as you perform feats of magic and alchemy that will arouse your conscious mind, and bring you to the eclipse of the moon, the circling of the stars and the field of dreams impossible.***

Take up your calling, find your light, finish what you have started and come with us.

The wisdom of the ancients need not grope in the dark unconsciousness of your mind to awaken you any longer.

Your time is in the hands of the now, provoking you to move swiftly onward.

No more waiting, no more hesitation, no more entanglements. Let us meet there soon, where you can realize that all is within plan and all is good."

I believe we six are like a microcosm of many such groups developing now. We are creating an energy field together. We are giving each other expanded power, allowing us to let go of old concepts and move into higher vibrations. Vibrations that ripple through our connections, touching us to move into higher elevated spaces. I would say this is the power of gatherings, communities and collectives. We will be better individuals because of it. We will benefit from it so all humanity can benefit and we can benefit from all humanity. The ones with light must lead the way. They must witness creation as a gift and this gift must not be held alone, rather shared, so the light can be shown upon a new Earth realized. Let us receive and be open. Let us relax and be carried. Let us be uplifted and be present to an aspect of our divine being, as it peeks through allowing itself to be known.

I understand that we are called to cultivate this connection with spirit and to remember we are these divine creators, each one of us a universe unto ourselves. We are at the portal leaning into our own awakenings as we come to witness the quantum field and the void of true existence.

> *The dimensions of the wheel of life revealed, as we step into no time of universal grace, as we float in the blackness without a hint of space, as we melt into the void where the quantum field sleeps to no end, as the silence that we've feared for so long sings, so strong, its universal love song, that we cannot deny this is where we come from and belong…*
>
> *As we realize death is but a new birthing of a soul torn as it merges back into its god form, and morning dawns yet again in the breath of a newborn's first cry… how can we possibly say we die?*

CHAPTER 15
Pickled Cucumbers

I guess you might have been waiting for me to ask, yet again, who is this god? I must say I was a bit afraid to ask, as this new realm I had been touching confused me and left me with questions I didn't know how to formulate. When I did inquire, this god came at me with a sideways bang that knocked me off my feet, surprising the heck out of me.

> *"I am the side view of the face of Yeshua. (Jesus)*
>
> *I am here to testify to the truth only love can provide. The essence of all being's material and non-material, is a divine love that carries with it the spark that creates all existence of form and non-form.*
>
> *Understand you are both. So, you may penetrate the world, your Earthly world, to make the changes needed to move*

from impending doom to an elevated enlightenment, to preserve what is left and grasp what is to come.

As you have heard, "the truth will set you free"…yes, but ahh! The truth combined with love will set you apart to ignite the Earth. To persuade the fires of destruction to morph into the flames of passion.

To mold the Earth. To shape the Earth, allowing the vibrations of the oneness of the universe to take you to other dimensions and realities, which are preparing for the transition awaiting you."

As you know I grew up in the city of Manhattan. It was called the concrete jungle implying that nature did not take precedence in our lives as we grew up there. So, you'll understand when I tell you a true life happening of mine which was extremely embarrassing, and one of those life lessons to be worked on.

In my early adult years with my husband, we moved from New York City to the suburbs of a small quaint town in New England. We would take walks in the evenings when he returned home from work. We would say to each other how monotonous these walks were, as all we saw were bushes and trees that looked unbearably the same. We used to love walking on paved streets in the city, with street lights and storefront windows to look in. So, for us, it seemed much less inviting.

I was feeling lonely then, still newly married but now with a child on my lap. We would sit on the front steps of our new home every afternoon without seeing anyone.

Until, finally one day I met a neighbor walking by. We started talking some and she invited me to come with her, just around the corner and up the street, for a cup of coffee and to see her garden. I can't tell you how my heart leapt to see more than trees and bushes coming at me in the form of a real live person. I jumped up, as best a 6-month pregnant mom holding her 10-month-old could, and started up the street, following her.

Her garden was beautiful with flowers and vegetables, tomatoes, squash, lettuce etc. I stood there wide-eyed as I pointed and said, "wow and you even grow pickles!" She laughed, as she smiled and said, "no, these are cucumbers". I immediately realized my mistake, blushing and laughing with her, but I never lived it down in that neighborhood or within myself - ugh!

As I look back, I realize just how much my husband and I were missing. We couldn't see the forest through the trees, as they say. Starting with those garden pickles and ending up not feeling what it is like to hug a tree, experience a leaf shower or smell a fresh mown field. I had started to experience an inkling of something on the land, during those years I spent at the Spiritual Life Center, but it would not come into focus for me for many years to come.

What do you want, I say?

I do not know, as mother Earth I cry.

But my children do not suck at my bosom's door, and their love is not felt anymore.

The panic is so real that even my being can feel where the pulse of my Earth may not heal.

How insane it seems to me now remembering that disconnect from her. My relationship with mother Earth is everything. Everything that comes in, and everything that goes out of me is from the Earth. We have been so domesticated by our society. We get food and water delivered to us making us forget the intrinsic nature of our planet body. I feel a longing, as many others do, to connect to this caring compassionate mother. To experience the taste of her milk while held in the stillness of her embrace. She continues to breathe life into me, as I now realize that she is a conscious, living, breathing organism. She gives us life and love unconditionally, as she moves with the tender rhythms of the universe. The truth is though, we are killing her! We have ravished her and there is no more getting away with murder!

This Yeshua speaks of a new Earth that will set us free. Not just me. Not just you. All material and non-material forms together for the purest intentions, burning with a cleansing fire of the pureness of love. Siphoning the old worn-out perspectives and illusions, so we may be present to the sucking of eternal wisdom, the gulping of loves nectar, and finally the tasting of humanities co-existence with awesome wonderment. The force of this energetic Godhead is none that I've ever experienced. Telling us our lives will collide with others joined with an explosion of fathomless kinship, of who we are as one. The knowledge of this will be the understanding of our evolution for all humanity to witness. For each individual to awaken to feel this presence and allow this extreme energy to burst forth within our bones, as we rest into the oneness of purpose.

I believe this God is asking us to unite and rotate with the Earth. So, we may feel the swirling energies spiraling in patterns that dizzy us with enthusiasm. A movement along divine lines and sacred patterns, opposite of chaos noticed only from our highest states. As our numbers mount and our consciousness expands, growing the momentum of this awakening, we will ultimately tip the balance that will empower our planet to move on to the next level of spiritual evolution.

We can greet this new dawning with great anticipation mindful of who we are. As the world twists and turns to transform and shows itself anew, attached to a reality of love and hope rather than revenge and war, I asked:

What do we need to know of this new mother Earth?

How do we help take this planet to its evolutionary openings?

"We are ready - we are here - we are you.

Create a new beginning standing on the shoulders of the old.

Look out from the shadows of chaos.

You are the seeds to spread, to grow, to produce a new humanity, with communities developing built in immune systems, that detect and eat fear before it enters and eats you.

As you go within, a new dimension will open to new streams of consciousness and new portals of expanded insights, opening to coherent fields of thought, allowing the capacity of your brain to enlarge and be filled with ever-expanding ideas.

You, as the gods of many, must merge together in perfect formation to become impenetrable.

To taste Gaia's exquisite bounty and sleep in the gardens of her love once again, as she bends toward the rhythmic pulsing of the universe."

CHAPTER 16
The Fragrance of a Feminine Spirit

You are my heartbeat.

You are the word.

You are the feminine Christ.

You are here to show the church its heart.

You are here to challenge it to survive.

It is dying without the woman.

Take your place as the mother of its soul.

Teach it how to carry its evolution.

Don't walk away, walk through.

> **Step out into a new paradigm. A new story transcending dogma and old rituals into the formation of a worldly movement of love. Rising in its intensity in itself to feel the softness of a woman's hands and the smile of a gentle soul, guiding its people to what the essence of the church's being rightly is…the beauty and fragrance of a feminine spirit sitting beside the plumage of graceful men. The shifting of the good news.**
>
> **Cry out, as these churches are set on fire to die in the ashes of the forgetfulness of their true essence, to rise to the light of the knowledge they are all one."**

Strike me once, strike me twice, strike me three times and you're out. That's the rule in baseball, three strikes and you're out: the Episcopal Church, the Metropolitan Community Church and the Spiritualist Church. I was sure I was finished, especially at my age. Instead, I'm hearing Tina Turner singing in my ear, "What's *age* got to do with it, got to do with it."

> **"You stand with me as this movement now has been happening with great frequency. You take the hands of those reaching for the center of their collective beings, witnessing each other in the unity of their spirits as one. To form a more perfect union, conscious**

as to who they are, why they are here, and what they have come to accomplish.

In this developed state of being, you sit with them, as you find them and they find you.

The spark ignited will find a new human collective forming, uniting other collectives all over the world. Communicating and flooding the Earth with new waters to drink and new plants to grow, to refresh, to nourish and to provide the taste and drink of a new abundance, a new beginning the world has yet to awaken to."

Oh my, yet another God to name in my tired state. Another voice I cannot deny nor turn away from. And ahh, dear me! … realizing this is a voice I've danced with before. The one that's been hounding me to come back. The voice from my childhood, but now stronger, touching me again in this mystical dance within my divine mind, yet somehow different. Jesus, the presence I grew up with. Jesus, the presence I fell in love with. Jesus, the presence I wrote poems about. Not that Jesus, the one I ran from. Not that false voice of the church, I prayed to never hear again. Not that voice I always felt hounded by. No, this was the voice of the true essence of the Cosmic Christ. The voice that was always pursuing me. A master guide. The master teacher of love that has been with me even in my being absent to it. As I look back, this universal God form undefined as a he or she, or of having a father in heaven, is the voice of the Christ-consciousness I've always been deeply aware of. I realize now that I have always been aligned with this consciousness all my life. And is why, even as a child, I knew and felt a rising state of compassion and love for all human- kind, even when I didn't act rightly to it.

You gave us hope, for in your voice was song and sun of a new life choice. And when I said I will, you jumped to your feet excited to be still.

It's not always in the actions or doings as some may say, rather in the attitude of compassion that holds your smile, that creates a new way.

CHAPTER 17
Never -Never Land

The period in my life during this covid pandemic pushing us into quarantine and quieting the Earth, allowed me to actually hear myself think. It also allowed the internal mechanisms of my mind to switch on to resonate with the hearings of my soul. Channelings came fast with enlightened awareness. But at times I would have trouble writing these hearings down, not understanding where they came from and leaving them overnight. As they seemed like such crazy ramblings, only to come back to read them the next day beguiled by their messages.

> *"A river flows in you, drink from it, sit in it, splash in it, hear its mumblings.*
>
> *As this is the river of your soul. Sip it, and taste the experiences, the source of your being.*

And, hold on for you will be taken to euphoric proportions, only felt by the holiest of holies tripping in the fantasies of the oneness of universal love.

Be it, see it, feel it, as we see you into a new way, a new dimension.

Our love will take you there."

As I heard this within my being, I realized this is the place where old polarities blend together into a harmony of oneness. A place where chaos, lack of safety and the absence of trust, no longer exist and we operate only from our inner guidance. A place that cannot be observed in a physical, tangible or direct manner. The saints called it the mystical dimension, while others now call it the 5th dimension. Either way, it is known to be a place where there are no words. A place we cannot show a picture of. A place that has no shape. A place where even the greatest minds cannot analyze it or present it in any form. It has to be an inner discovery. A discovery found in simplicity and beauty of one's own self, reflecting every being, every river within our minds and every fold and scar in the universe. Here, we might recognize ourselves as transient beings traveling within our bodies. Beings like Peter Pan and Tinker-Bell in Never- Never Land, flying in ships to new worlds to anchor in the forests of entanglement. Where the food of thought and the drink of awareness can capture our souls to free our sin-sick minds, as we fly out to sprinkle fairy dust throughout the galaxies. Yes, crazy, as it may seem, we are flying in the light of the sun, swimming in the Earthly Sea of confusion and drinking in the wild air of life, as we delight in the expansion of our souls.

Here we are trying to understand further about this new reality we are working towards. I found a trance-channeler on-line, Asil Toksal, giving a course on ascension. He was speaking about the quantum field, our higher dimensional selves and accessing the collective oneness. I took this workshop and realized it was about increasing our frequencies in order to raise the frequency of the collective oneness. And raising the Earth's vibrations, forming at this time a movement to bring us into the next evolutionary dimension. Wow!!

And I realized through these courses and Asil's channellings that we are on the verge of so much more than we can imagine. We are on the edge of tomorrow where we can feast on the energies that are rising on this planet, as the age of polarity is being replaced with the age of wholeness/oneness. This outmoded template of polarity is breaking down. Its low frequency vocabulary, full of negative and warrior words, is beginning to give way to a new and balanced form of collective human empowerment. We are the ones we've been waiting to encounter. We are the ones we've been hungering to meet to call us out of the wilderness. We are the voice of our dreams. We are responsible for marrying science with spirituality, as we work within the realms of such things as sacred geometry, quantum physics, and metaphysics to continue to pull back the veil, to greet this field of unending possibilities.

> *We are thought.*
> *We are expression.*
> *We are expansion.*
> *We cannot be less.*
> *We cannot be other.*
> *We cannot be extinguished.*
> *We are eternal.*
> *We are sacred.*
> *We are divine.*
> *We are them.*
> *We are you.*
> *We are me.*

There is no more seeking. There is only the alchemy of love, creating the "we" into existence. The molding of our beings into this human form, so we may enter into this Earthly reality, albeit, but for a mere moment in time, to experience the consciousness of universal love. I feel as though I'm in and out of growth and expansion here and my head is spinning in some kind of crazy orbit on this mystical track. My emotions are constantly in flux on this winding path of evolution. And my heart is skipping its normal beat at times seemingly taking on the rhythm of my soul. We are quickening, as the Earth's energies are intensifying to create waves of increasing adjustments for us to receive these energies with grace. The rise of globalism is swallowing the extreme antagonists and those who stagnate in the silence of mediocrity, so we may thrive as we protect the Earth; as we walk into a new reality, a new renaissance of unimaginable beauty connected to a culture of harmony, love and peace.

> *My mind in meditation is like a feather floating back and forth in the air, no tripping, no stopping all silent movement, that's all it can bear.*
>
> *Until it rests in the mind of my heart, tickling it to open as it passes to start the seeds of ecstatic compulsion there, to settle into a consciousness*
>
> *I have yet to be aware.*
>
> *As my breathe pushes it softly into gentle explosion of a fancy of new feathers commencing to do the same,*
>
> *I am taken on a ride of universal magnitude from whence I came.*

I am perceiving the sounds that we are here to bring light to those who believe that this world is all it seems to be. To those who trust that what they see is all that they will get. And to those who accept what they experience daily is their only reality. We are here to bring people hope that think the world needs war and violence to combat the fears brought about from all sorts of iniquities, and who continuously fan the flames of aggression.

My heart is crying out as my eyes bleed with tears asking to please look further into who we truly are. We don't have to play the unfriendly games any longer. We don't need to chew on the bones of others to be free of fear. This world has shown us more. It has shown us the magic of love and the mysteries of conscious awakenings. We have found wondrous potential in our humanness through such things as, realizing the heart too has a brain, the higher vibrations of love can renew and heal our bodies, and our minds are capable of touching the minds of others in different parts of the world without physically being there. If we can accomplish all this and so much more:

Couldn't we believe we could study peace as we work through our aggressions.

Couldn't we believe we could finally dictate a new story.

Couldn't we believe we could challenge our blindness to visualize new ways to fill the Earth with flowers of kindness.

Couldn't we believe we could dispel the lies of being powerless, and beat down the doors of hypocrisy and vile claims that we are insignificant.

Couldn't we believe that we are enough. More than enough. To be able to heighten our vibrations to rip the veil of ignorance from our eyes, feeling certain that we could lift the veil of wisdom to reveal the promise of enlightenment that the universe has set before us.

We are not incontinent beings having to be led by the relentless stalking's of immoral and wicked people who have malformed and malicious minds. Wisdom is about being able to put situations into perspective, with an ability to discern from our inner guidance how to process the movements necessary for us to advance. So, we can stand like a force of nature as the activities on this planet rise to activate our ascension templates, allowing us to move beyond today and into a collective evolutionary moment.

CHAPTER 18

Unlimited Possibilities

A friend recently posed this question to me: what is your reality? When I dove deep inside my mind for an answer, I went into a tailspin. Some believe that this life is an illusion and possess various theories as to the relevance of that illusion. Hmm, so what is my reality? Pausing to think more deeply, I was guided to reflect on a strange event that happened to me many years ago concerning my first spiritual mentor.

It was during my experience in AA, while still a young mother. Apparently, I had overwhelmed my sponsor, making her dizzy with my deluge of questions over several months about how she viewed the world. It was suggested that I go to see a Dominican nun, Sister Mary Victoria, for the wisdom that I sought. Little did I realize at the time that these questions fit into the world of metaphysics.

Sister Mary V, as I called her, lived in a cloistered monastery a mere mile from my house. She was given special permission to see me this one time, after the pleadings of my sponsor. The nuns were committed to living in seclusion for the purpose of prayer. I was truly frightened as I walked through those heavy front doors. My heart skipped a beat as I was directed to sit in a partitioned room behind a waist-high beautiful hard wood barrier. Unaccustomed to this level of formality, though thoroughly exposed to its traditiion, I felt a bit spooked. Sister Mary V then arrived and took her seat in the chair across from this divide. Something inside me shifted. I was jolted with the realization that I was in the presence of a holy woman. Bowing my head in response to her gaze, she smiled generously, seeing my uncomfortable demeanor and said, "Good morning." I timidly smiled back and said, "I'm not entirely sure why I'm here!" Her reply started me on a journey that I have not yet fully integrated. "Are you asking, why are you here in this world?"

I was with her for a mere hour and a half, yet upon leaving, I knew that the depth of love and compassion that she displayed to me had changed my very being. This time, I was the dizzy one walking home with my heart still pounding, and with a feeling of sadness because I had not a clue where to turn. I knew that I needed help to continue to understand and articulate these profound feelings that Sister Mary V had fully awakened in me. Where do I go now with these "profound somethings" that I have begun to touch?

Over the next few days, it felt impossible to perform the ordinary duties of cooking, cleaning and performing the likes of maintaining everything material. The only thing that eased the sadness of living within this cloud of perceived disparity, between the spiritual and the physical that was my daily life, were my children. They'd return home from school, glowing with excitement, eager to entertain me with the happenings of their day, like stars shining through the darkness. Little did I know in these moments, that the Universe was conspiring on my behalf and that the help I needed was on its way!

To my utter surprise, one week later, I was summoned back to the monastery to see Sister Mary V a second time. And though not certain of why I was summoned, an energy that can only be described as joyful hope poured into me. When next I saw her, she explained that she had spoken with the Mother Superior about our initial visit, and was then granted permission to see me once a week for an hour to offer spiritual direction. For the first time in my life, I didn't question this offering. Instead, I allowed myself to be in awe and acceptance of this sacred opportunity.

Our conversations quickly went from my asking multiple questions to being the one questioned. I can positively say without hesitation, that this is when my spiritual journeying seriously took roots. During those two years of regular sessions, the world of mysticism grew more real within me, until it was time to truly spread my wings and fly. The last time I saw Sister Mary V, when we spoke about my ending the sessions, I noticed a golden light that formed around her entire being. Rubbing my eyes to validate this reality, she continued to radiate pure golden light and I knew that I truly was in the presence of an angel.

Many years later, while walking to the store, I bumped into a woman that I barely knew. Approaching me she stated, "Hey, you know Sister Mary V, right?" She then proceeded to inform me that Sister Mary V had had a heart attack and was most likely dying as we spoke. I thanked her and continued walking with a saddened heart, knowing I wouldn't be permitted to see her. She would be in the cloister surrounded by her sisters, singing her sweetly to sleep, whilst drifting towards the heavenly realms. But I did want to tell her how much she meant to me. The woman turned and called to me again to say that Sister Mary V, oddly enough, was out of the cloister. She was in a nursing home nearby and that I might want to go see her. I couldn't imagine why she would be out of the monastery, but more importantly I knew I did want to go to visit her. She and I had spoken many times about this eventuality; about her becoming sick or dying one day and how her family wouldn't be able to be present, much less myself. Standing there stunned for about five minutes, I decided that I was going anyway, fully aware that, at least one or two other sisters would be there sitting vigil and would refuse to let me enter her room.

I arrived at the nursing home and approached the nurse's station, where I was told that she was in the last room down the hall. Walking down the dimly lit corridor, I came in contact with no one. I entered her room and was startled to see that Sister Mary V was alone, lying in bed, seemingly unconscious. She was not attired in the familiar white habit and her veil laid on the nightstand with her rosary beads. This caught me as totally bizarre. I stood there, again stunned for a moment. Knowing that she would be appalled by her appearance, I picked up a brush and began stroking her hair. Sister Mary V had always been so proper pushing back any loose strands of hair, up inside her veil. I then was able to tell her how much she meant to me. How I still heard her voice telling me about the mysteries of the universe she had discovered and how she never dismissed one question of mine. I picked up her rosary beads and put them in her hands, wanting to pray the rosary with her once more. We had always done that, so many years ago, while driving to her doctor's appointments. Back then, I would start the car and she would start the rosary. I would stop the car and she would stop the rosary. On the way home, we would drive past a deli that she loved. Of course, unbeknownst to anyone else, I would stop and buy her a sandwich. We would continue on, Sister Mary V silent, except for the occasional sound of smacking lips while I talked about my life. When she was done, we laughed as I collected the wrappings to discard any evidence. She then picked up her rosary again and we prayed the remainder of the trip back to the monastery, as if never missing a beat.

I sat by her bedside, with my own rosary in hand and started with the joyful mysteries. My eyes widened and my heart skipped a beat, as I saw her fingers move along her beads. Finishing our prayers, I stood up, leaving the beads in her hands. I kissed her forehead and said goodbye.

I have since told many friends and family about this unexpected encounter, with tears in my eyes and a gratitude unlike any other I'd experienced.

Yet, until recently acquainted with the concept of multiple realities, I was unable to shake off the illusion that this could never have happened. None of the sisters leave the cloister when actively dying and if they did, they would be accompanied by other nuns. Then it hit me. This encounter with her actually never did happened. This felt so real and yet for many reasons, it could not have happened on this physical plane. In that moment of Sister Mary V's passing, I had entered into another realm that was as real as the one I had been in moments before, but different. In this simultaneous reality, I experienced a mystical encounter held out of time and space, and outside of the limitations of what we call a normal experience. For a moment of pure grace, it showed me that we are all on an eternal loop moving in and out of various realities. I knelt in utmost gratitude and continue to do so, in awe of this capacity that we all have to experience moments like these at any time. My perception of reality was changed forever.

So, I can tell you from that experience that I believe reality is not static; rather it is fluid and offers each of us unlimited possibilities. In my experience, reality shifts as often as my thoughts change, based on my perspective. Similar to how my perception of God's keep changing and growing. It seems to me that our reality is constantly in flux. When we see the world as a child, we see it differently than as an adult. My reality, as I wrote and breathed life into this book, changed almost with each new page. And, even if I wanted to stop and wait for the next word, in that silence a new word would present itself to challenge a new perspective, possibly giving way to a new reality. And, realizing with another "aha" moment in the journey of my life, it was just another thing that I couldn't touch or control.

Reality slips through our fingers at every turn and plays games as we chase it, as we try to catch and hold onto it. Inevitably, it disappoints us to no end. It is elusive and brings new awakenings, whether they be light or dark, allowing us to be caught in the moments of old habits or within the spaces of our unique fears. These shadowy places within us present themselves now more than ever, to be touched by the new patterns of light that are reflecting through the prisms of our souls. Maybe one could say, reality is that fleeting perception you catch out of the corner of your eye. Perhaps it's the antecedent of a transformation, as we are held in the oneness of the universe. I am blessed to now be aware that my life is a flowing reality within the dream of God. Understanding to a fuller extent with each breath I take, that I can walk in this God consciousness. Further revealing to myself, as others also reveal to me, that we are one, expressing universal God energy. Maybe this is truly where heaven meets Earth. The gratitude in my heart cannot be matched with words, as the feelings of this passionate love of the divine that I experienced as a young child has come round full circle, to meet me again in my twilight years. All the searching, wandering, and learning have brought me thus far, to a comfortable peace and harmonious state, allowing me to experience a field where all things are created anew. Existing, at least for some moments, in time.

CHAPTER 19

The Hidden Milk of Everlastingness

I've been told, taking all things into consideration that … I am.

I am me. I am one with the universe, with no limitations, with no sense of turning back. And, if this is so I will squander this time and look out into the universe and say…come, come get me and do with me as you will. Move me gently one atom at a time, or move me with a force that moves my atoms to explode within me and out into this world. I used to want to know where I was going and what your name is. I would even beg you to find out. But now it doesn't matter, for I'm certain that no *matter* stands still nor ever remains the same. Your name is eternally whispered into every expanding heart. Aligning in intimate resonance with each beat so that we can call your name from wherever we stand.

Some years back I tried my hand in past life regression therapy with the renowned Brian Weiss and quickly realized that I needed to immerse myself more deeply into hypnotic techniques. This modality fascinated me. I consistently witnessed the presence of my higher self in these sessions guiding my clients to specific past events, that would lead to the insights needed for them to reconcile with life. Witnessing how my clients were always influenced to greater insights within themselves made me wish to be always available to continue in this amazing field.

I then completed a 100-hour course from the University of Florida School of Hypnosis. I gained much knowledge and from that knowledge realized that I was actually led to the study of hypnosis because, I desired to discover the mysterious insights within my own soul. When I finally discerned this, I sought out Dolores Cannon's Quantum Healing Hypnosis Techniques Academy (QHHT). I was drawn there from the information I read as to the way one could ask questions of their superconscious, their divine-self, their soul and have it answer. This not only intrigued me but brought me to the recognition that meditation was a form of hypnosis. Questions one might ask in this state regarding our divine self could indeed be answered. I slowly began to understand why we don't have to do much more than this to enter into our conscious awareness of the quantum field. This is the field of limitless openings. What some physicists might call the fifth dimensional field, where matter explodes into particles of unending possibilities. I found my mind immersed, soaking in this wild discovery of a non-dualistic collective oneness and the emancipation from senseless thoughts. I continued my studies in this field and met a world of thought that I had never conceived before was possible beyond sci-fi books and movies.

So, maybe in some small way I was coming to actualize for myself the alpha and the omega of universal thought, were there is no beginning and no end. We gaze up to the stars looking for a piece of the universal puzzle. One that will answer the questions sought by every being that travels by to touch the wonderment of this Earthly world. What is my purpose and why am I here?

My way of viewing things has changed throughout my 75 years. My religious beliefs have changed from Christianity and not knowing what to call my God, to studying many other religions. And in most religions and philosophies seeing the good as well as the sameness in them. From universality to psychic perspectives, to channeling, to the healing of science connecting with spirituality…

I don't hold any tightly now, as I throw caution to the wind and ride side saddle laughing at myself, taking life a little lighter, realizing I am graced to find the oneness that all of life has in common. That we are all expressions of one divine breath.

The breath that gives us purpose and is explicit and exquisite in its callings to eternal truths, and mindful meanderings.

The breath that gives us the freedom of movement to soar into the nothingness of oneness.

The breath that gives us the network placing our essence in the hands of a more intricate knowing.

The breath that gives us the spirit to sing a song of a passionate love, allowing us to hear the music of many souls.

The breath that leads us to the self-realization of purpose, and the reason we are being enveloped in this Earthly cocoon of nature and nurture.

The breath that gives us the awareness, of feeling the true infusion of our being in service to the constant call of the collective oneness.

So, I now can see naming you is only for my comfort and release for me to find some peace.

What would I expect to gain there's nothing else to take the rein.

So, naming me is where I need to be to allow myself to flow into an unending sea of divine remembrance, as I stand on human ground to know what I have found.

The tender love within my breast to expel the hidden milk of everlastingness.

For others to recognize this in themselves as they too walk the land awaken to who they are and why they've come thus far.

To take it further pushing onward to ascend the coarseness and harshness of a world that must mend, becoming what it was intended to be… a living, breathing conscious form of a mysterious/mystical reality.

Dying to myself once again and finding yet another God that can remain nameless, I travel onward with the tenderness and fragility of a being living in the wisdom of her age.

Knowing that in this time of accelerated growth on Earth I can still have a place with other aging beings. To help unlock the old antiquated ways and become a radical midwife of souls birthing into this new reality.

Within this new potential I can watch and experience as science bumps into spirituality. Exploding with the force of the big bang propelling us further into the future on this magical, mystical energy tour only the stars have an awareness of…

Time, I thought you were my friend, but now I know you are more as you walk me to the end.

My name is Pat (Cookie). When someone asks where I live, I don't say I live in Florida or Massachusetts. Heck no, I just say I live in the field of never-ending possibilities! I'll meet you there!

EPILOGUE

What do you want from this world?

An apple or a pear, an adventure or a dare.

A quiet walk, or a run without care.

What do you want from this world?

A place to plant your feet,

or a pad from which to leap

or is it the freedom to grasp it all even if you fall,

from the heights of ecstasy to the depths of despair,

knowing you are privileged just to be there.

In the Terrain of the Now, always able to click your heels to find your home when you fear you are alone. Coming to rest from afar or above, within your being, knowing you are blessed, to follow the doves within the heart of your love.

As I started out writing this book, I had no realization as to what I was supposed to say or who I was actually writing this book for. In a state of acute confusion at first, I began typing words and sentences from my mind, my heart, my soul or ... What!? They just poured out of me, onto the pages. Now you'll know, that I didn't write this book. It wrote me! I'm still in awe of it and the wisdom it found within me. For truly, little did I know what laid within my soul. But more to the point, I discovered that all this wisdom lies within your soul as well, although uniquely your own and likely even more awesome and mystical!

> "*The veil within your heart has been lifted for you to now experience more fully how close we are.*
>
> *Take my hand and come float with us to the distant land of abundant souls.*
>
> *A land no human being can imagine in flesh, but can come to feel, where the pulse of all souls is made one.*
>
> *Where all love is formed into a universal mass of oneness connecting all the stars, planets, solar systems and galaxies - ever expanding to embrace the importance of YOU!*

Yes, You, for without you a vacuum would present itself in the collective fabric and discord would ensue.

We want you to understand your importance within the oneness of all things. No one can be replaced.

This cannot be mistaken, for this is why you are here.

As the fabric of Mother Earth is weakening, the time has come for the people to unite, and create a vibrational boundary to protect the Earth.

Your energies are needed to develop a new paradigm, building fresh relationships so that all may see through each other's eyes the framework of this evolutionary shift, and love each other into your next dimension.

We are here to help you all bring a quiet peacefulness to your soul, allowing you the courage to move beyond your knowing into the landscape of limitless possibilities.

We ask that you hear us and can rest in our favors."

I want to take my hands and hold each face that's touched me in this lifetime, to look straight into their eyes and thank them for teaching me. Each interaction whether experienced as favorable or as a struggle was beneficial for my growth, and helped to form the woman that I have come to be.

Strange how things take on a new perspective as time goes on. We can see with new eyes that shine brightly from within, capturing the shadows of our thoughts and shifting our consciousness to new heights. We have the potential to grow wiser from every involvement. Could it be then, that through the course of writing this book, I've more fully integrated my past and let go of any negative false narratives still buried in my mind? So many memories have flooded out from my heart and soul.

My desire is that, as you read this book, YOU will experience more of that something that seems to exist just outside of our minds. That touch of... is it, grace? that will free your mind and touch more deeply the truth within your own heart. That you will discover something so enchanting and mysterious, that it will lead you to a new dimension for your own expansion. One that is full of power and love and the source of all possibilities.

And, should you wish, will you continue to stretch with me, to that place where we can all taste colors and see music and feast on radiance and light? And when anyone ask us where we're from, we won't say Earth. We'll say we are from the stars! See you there!

www.ingramcontent.com/pod-product-compliance
Lightning Source LLC
LaVergne TN
LVHW011716060526
838200LV00051B/2919